Peter Augustus Porter

**A Brief History of Old Fort Niagara**

Peter Augustus Porter

**A Brief History of Old Fort Niagara**

ISBN/EAN: 9783743353732

Manufactured in Europe, USA, Canada, Australia, Japa

Cover: Foto ©ninafisch / pixelio.de

Manufactured and distributed by brebook publishing software (www.brebook.com)

Peter Augustus Porter

**A Brief History of Old Fort Niagara**

# A BRIEF HISTORY

OF

# OLD FORT NIAGARA

BY
PETER A. PORTER.

PHOTOGRAPHS BY ORRIN E. DUNLAP.

NIAGARA FALLS.
1896.

COPYRIGHT, 1896, BY PETER A. PORTER.

**MADE IN**
THE COMPLETE ART-PRINTING WORKS
OF
THE MATTHEWS-NORTHRUP CO.
BUFFALO, N. Y.

17022

THIS SKETCH

OF THE

HISTORY OF OLD FORT NIAGARA

IS INSCRIBED TO THE MEMORY OF

ORSAMUS H. MARSHALL,

THE HISTORIAN OF THE NIAGARA FRONTIER,

AT WHOSE SUGGESTION

THE AUTHOR COMMENCED THE STUDY

OF THE

HISTORY OF THIS LOCALITY.

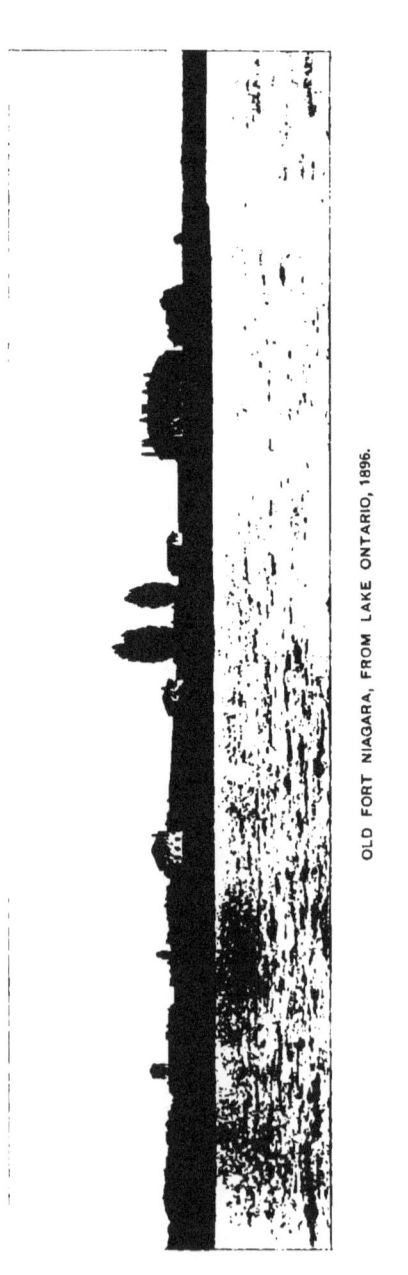

OLD FORT NIAGARA, FROM LAKE ONTARIO, 1896.

OLD FORT NIAGARA, FROM CANADA, 1896.

# INTRODUCTION.

THE TITLE of this pamphlet, read literally, correctly states the aim of the author. His desire has been to write a "BRIEF" history of "OLD" Fort Niagara.

Of the history of "modern" Fort Niagara, that is, from 1825, since which time it has not been considered a defensive work, no attempt has been made to treat.

Numerous authorities have been quoted in support of historical facts; many more might have been quoted. To those who read this article from a desire to study the history of Fort Niagara these references will be valuable. It has also been thought desirable to make liberal quotations from documents and books referred to.

OLD FORT NIAGARA, FROM THE LIGHT HOUSE.

# A BRIEF HISTORY OF OLD FORT NIAGARA.

NIAGARA is without exception the most important post in America and secures a greater number of communications, through a more extensive country, than perhaps any other pass in the world." So wrote Mr. Wynne in 1770,[1] and he undoubtedly expressed the opinion which both the French and the English then held and had held for the preceding hundred years.

For probably no one spot of land in North America, the Heights of Quebec and the lower end of Manhattan Island alone excepted, had played so important a part, been so coveted and exerted so great an influence, both in peace and war, on the control, on the growth, on the settlement and on the civilization of the country, as this little point of land at the mouth of and on the eastern shore of the Niagara River, bounded on one side by that river and on the other side by Lake Ontario.

And both Quebec and Manhattan Island had been settled for half a century before La Salle first saw this spot, whose importance as a strategic point, in peace, in war, and in the interest of the fur trade he at once recognized; and as from La Salle came the first suggestion of a fort here, with his name must its earliest history be forever linked.

And for nearly one hundred years after La Salle's first visit, the ministers and statesmen of both France and England, backed by all the power of their respective kingdoms, aided by their armies, their great generals and all their experienced colonial officers from the highest to the lowest, made the possession and fortification of this small piece of land one of the main objective points of their respective policies regarding their American possessions.

The Niagara River "Onguiaahra, the famous river of the Neuter Nation," had been well known to the Jesuit missionaries as early as

[1] British Empire in America, vol. II, page 102. Note.

1640,[1] and by hearsay since at least 1626; and the fact that a great fall interrupted the passage of the Indians on their westward journeys had been announced by Lescarbot in his "Histoire de la Nouvelle France," published in 1609,[2] in his description of Cartier's second voyage to America, made in 1535.

And it was the knowledge of a carrying place around these falls that pointed out to those engaged in, and ambitious to control, the fur trade with the Western Indians, in which list La Salle stands out prominently, that a fortified store house at or near the end of this portage would be a priceless advantage to its possessors.

And during the long period above referred to when France and England were making every effort to gain control of this locality, the fur traders rendered valuable services in furtherance of the ambitions of their respective nations, although, of course, these fur traders' object was a purely mercenary one.

But the Indians, prompted thereto partly by the always enduring feuds between the Huron and Iroquois stocks, but mainly by their keen insight into the real ambitions of the white men — faithful and friendly to the French and the English alternately, but only as fear of their strength or benefits to be derived from them impelled — clearly foresaw the danger to their race if a stronghold was ever obtained at the portage, and persistently refused to allow one to be erected; and it was only after a struggle of 50 years that France succeeded in getting near this spot a fortified structure, that promised to be, and though soon after removed seven miles distant to the mouth of the river, proved to be, a permanency.

### THE INDIAN TITLE TO THE LAND.

In tracing the history of Fort Niagara, it is desirable for us, especially so far as the earliest claims of ownership of the territory in which it is located by France and England, are concerned, to look first at the Indian title to the land and their disposition thereof.

As far back as we can get any authentic knowledge whatsoever the Neuter Nation owned and occupied this spot. They were probably a powerful offshoot from the great Huron-Iroquois stock, and occupied all the territory north of Lake Erie from near the Detroit River eastward until their lands met those of the Iroquois near the Genesee River.

[1] Jesuit Relation, published 1642, page 49. [2] Page 382.

The Neuters derived their name from the fact that, while often at war with other tribes, they never warred with either the Iroquois or Hurons, between whom they were located. They counted 36 villages west of the Niagara River and four east of it,[1] and were a well-built and populous nation.

Such a neutrality could not last, and while we do not know when the Neuters first became recognized as an independent nation (certainly before 1600, for in 1615 Champlain refers to them as an established tribe), we do know that it was in 1651 that the Senecas, the most westerly, the strongest numerically, as well as the most bloodthirsty of the Iroquois, attacked them on a slight pretext, and in a short and bloody campaign wiped them out of existence as a nation, the remnant that was spared being incorporated among their captors.

The Senecas thenceforth, although it was over a hundred years before they occupied the Neuters' territory, claimed title to it by reason of this conquest, and among the Indian tribes the Senecas' claim seems to have been fully recognized.

For, as we shall see later on, the Senecas granted La Salle important rights on the Niagara River in 1679.

In 1719 they gave Joncaire, a Frenchman who had been adopted into their nation, certain rights on this river, which were of direct benefit to the French, and refused equal rights to the English; and, in 1725, they consented to the French building a stone fort at the mouth of the river.

The Senecas, in common with all other Indian tribes, seem to have regarded their land deeds and their treaties as binding only so long as it suited their convenience. Again, some of their deeds embrace huge tracts of land, occupied by several tribes, the sachems or chiefs of which all joined in the deed of the whole territory, not specifying what portion each tribe owned.

Those deeds that embrace the locality we are treating of, of course, bear on the subject in hand.

### CONFLICTING CLAIMS.

Both France and England at an early date set up and steadily claimed title among other territory to this special locality.

France, by reason generally of early discoveries and occupation by Champlain (who never was on the Niagara River), by Coureurs de Bois, by Jesuit missionaries and later by La Salle.

[1] Jesuit relation, published 1642, pages 48 and 49.

England claiming the whole continent by reason of its discovery by her early navigators, (who were not the first discoverers of the continent,) maintaining a claim by the grant from James I. to Gorges, in 1620, of the land from ocean to ocean, and from 40 to 48 degrees of latitude, and by other, though conflicting grants, none of them made good by occupation or actual sovereignty, and by her conquest of the Dutch at Manhattan.

Parkman, writing of the period (1687) when French and English came in contact in the Senecas' territory, and set up their rival claims, says, "It is clear that the claim of prior discovery and occupation was on the side of the French."[1]

Both the French and English claimed the Iroquois as subjects, but the Senecas especially always claimed independence.

### DEEDS FROM THE SENECAS.

In 1684, the five nations gave England a protectorate over their lands,[2] and in 1686 the English governor at New York set up the Duke of York's arms in all the castles of the Five Nations "as far as Oneigra."[3] In 1687 the Five Nations assented, when James II. of England agreed to accept them as his subjects.[4]

In 1701, the Senecas and other tribes deeded to William III., King of England, in trust a territory 800 miles by and 400 miles broad, "including, likewise, the Great Falls Oakinagaro."[5] The deed is signed by the totems of sachems of all the Five Nations.

In 1726, the Senecas again deeded in trust to the English king a large tract of territory, including "all along the River of Oniagara."[6]

But all these deeds seem to have been regarded even by the English grantees as of little value, and it was not till 1764, as noted later on, that a specific deed of a comparatively small area of country, being that along both banks of the Niagara River, was regarded as perfect, and was recognized as finally transferring to the English the Indian title to this famous region.

While Parkman, as above quoted, may be right as to the superiority of the French claims, by reason of prior discovery and occupation, if there was any right of title to this land in the Senecas, (and I believe there was,) by conquest, the English certainly seem to have acquired at an early date, by deeds from the Indians, what they after-

---

[1] Parkman, Frontenac and New France, page 161. [2] Col. Docs. N. Y., vol III, page 508. [3] Col. Docs. N. Y., vol. III, page 396. [4] Col. Docs. N. Y., vol. III, page 503 [5] Col. Docs. N. Y., vol IV, page 909. [6] Col. Docs. N. Y., vol V, page 800.

wards acquired by arms from the French, namely, the title to the land where Fort Niagara now stands.

### HISTORIC PERIODS.

Recognizing, therefore, the title to the spot where Fort Niagara stands as vested in the Senecas after their conquest of the Neuters in 1651, we may divide its history into the following periods:

Indian ownership, 1651–1669; Indian ownership, French influence predominating, 1669–1725; Indian ownership, French occupation, 1725–1759; Indian ownership, English occupation, 1759–1764; English ownership and occupation, 1759–1783; American ownership. English occupation, the "Hold-over Period," 1783–1796; American ownership and occupation, (excepting December 19, 1813, to March 27, 1815,) 1796–1896.

Let us now take up this history in chronological order.

### LA SALLE'S FIRST VISIT.

In 1669, La Salle, in company with Dollier de Casson and René de Gallinee, set out from Quebec for the Mississippi, and in his journal Gallinee tells of their passing near the mouth of the Niagara River and speaks of the Falls whose roar they heard,[1] this being the earliest known description of our Cataract. This date is generally accepted as that of La Salle's first visit to this section.

Opposed to this, however, is the official statement of the Marquis de Nonville, dated July 31, 1687, that "La Salle had erected quarters at Niagara in 1668, which quarters were burnt by the Senecas 12 years ago,"[2] that is in 1675.

To my mind De Nonville, writing 18 years after La Salle's visit, made an error of one year, and should have written 1669. We know that La Salle was here in 1669, and a few days later was with his two companions above named at an Indian village near the present city of Hamilton, Canada, and here he met Joliet, who was on his way back to Quebec from Lake Superior.[3]

Separating from his two companions at this village September 30, 1669, we next hear of La Salle "continuing his way on a river which goes from east to west, and passes to Onondaga, then to six or seven leagues below Lake Erie,"[4] conceded to be the Ohio.

[1] O. H. Marshall's writings, page 219, he quotes Gallinee's Journal.  [2] Doc. Hist. N. Y., vol. I, pages 150–1.  [3] O. H. Marshall's writings, page 223.  [4] J. G. Shea, Bursting of Margry's Bubble, page 16, he refers to Margry.

In order to reach the Ohio La Salle must have retraced his steps eastward, and thus either crossed or passed the mouth of the Niagara River.

He had several men with him; he may have tarried on the Niagara; he may have visited the Falls; he probably built the quarters of which De Nonville tells. If he did build them, there is no reason why the Senecas should not have burnt them as stated.

Certain it is that when La Salle returned to this locality in January, 1679, as described later on, he knew the country thoroughly; he knew just where to land ; he intended to build a fort here ; he knew about the Falls, and he came with the intention, and fully prepared to build a vessel above them. It is, therefore, I submit, possible, and even probable, that in this unrecorded interval above referred to La Salle made a careful study of the surroundings here, and built the house to which De Nonville refers.

## LA SALLE'S SECOND VISIT.

In 1678, La Salle projected an expedition to the far West, and on November 18th, of that year, La Motte, Hennepin and fourteen others started from Fort Frontenac in a brigantine of 10 tons for Niagara, and on the 6th of December they rounded the point where Fort Niagara now stands, and anchored their vessel in "the beautiful River Niagara, which no bark had ever yet entered."[1]

On this point of land was a fishing village of the Senecas, white fish then, as now, being abundant in the river at this spot.[2] All the land was covered with a dense thicket. On this point of land, on December 11, 1678, Hennepin said the first mass that had ever been celebrated in this territory.[3] In a letter written by him to the Prince de Conti, dated October 31, 1678, just before Hennepin and his comrades sailed, La Salle wrote that Tonti, who was to accompany him, was setting out to build a new fort 200 leagues away, near Niagara Falls, to which he (La Salle) had taken the liberty to give the name of Fort Conti.[4]

The vessel and crew remained at this spot from the 6th to the 15th of December, and the carpenters were at work.[5]

"It is at the mouth of Lake Frontenac (Ontario) that a fort was begun," wrote Hennepin,[6] "but the Iroquois took umbrage, so that, as

[1] Hennepin, Louisiana, 1683, page 23.  [2] Hennepin, Louisiana, 1683, page 32.  [3] Hennepin, Louisiana, 1683, page 24.  [4] Parkman, Discovery of the Great West, page 118.  [5] Hennepin, New Discovery, 1698, page 50.  [6] Hennepin, Louisiana, 1683, page 30.

we were not in a position to resist them, we contented themselves with building there a house defended by palisades, which is called Fort Conti, and the place is naturally defensive, and beside it there is a very fine harbor for barks to retire to in security."[1]  In a later work he adds that it was built on the east side of the Niagara River at its mouth.[2] Prevented from erecting a regular fort at the mouth of the River, La Motte, acting probably under explicit instructions from La Salle, took his vessel and crew up the river, to where Lewiston now stands, where he wanted to erect a store-house. His orders evidently were to try and build a fort at the mouth of the river; failing in that — as he had — to build a store-house at the foot of the portage, which would aid him in the fur trade, which the Indians might permit, and which would give a foothold, and could be used as trading-post, and gradually fortified, till such time as a real fort could be built and maintained at the river's mouth. If these were La Salle's plans, and I believe they were, he only anticipated history by some fifty years, for, as will be seen later, it was by this very plan and on this very spot that the French ultimately built a fortified store-house of some pretentions, which served all their purposes, military and commercial, till they obtained permission to build a stone fort on the coveted point of land.

On the site of Lewiston La Motte's men built their cabin, fortified with palisades,[3] using hot water to thaw the frozen ground. Here La Salle soon joined them. He had left Fort Frontenac some time after La Motte's departure, for the site of his projected Fort Conti at the mouth of the Niagara River, but, narrowly escaping shipwreck, landed at the mouth of the Genesee River. He visited the chief Seneca village, met the chiefs, and obtained from them their consent, (which, but a few days before, they had refused to La Motte and Hennepin,) to the building of a vessel above the cataract and the establishing of a fortified warehouse at the mouth of the river.[4]

His first work was the building of his vessel above the Falls, and after having located the place of building, and having seen the keel laid, he led a sergeant and a number of men to the mouth of the river, in order at once to take advantage of the Senecas' consent to

---
[1] Hennepin, Louisiana, 1683, page 31.  [2] Hennepin, Nouville Decouverte, 1697, page 48.
[3] Parkman, La Salle and Discovery of Great West. page 126, he quotes Tonty, Relation, 1684, Margry, vol. I, page 573  Tonti, La Salle's Last Discoveries, 1698, page 20.
[4] Parkman, La Salle and Discovery of the Great West, page 128, be quotes Letter de La Salle, Margry, vol. II. page 32.

his building a fortified warehouse there — a project specially dear to his heart.

Here on the famous point of land, in February, 1679, La Salle marked out the foundations of two block-houses,[1] set his men to work, and started on foot for Fort Frontenac.

In accordance with his promise to that Prince, he called these block-houses Fort Conti. They seemed to have been finished and occupied, but after a few months — probably about July, — through the carelessness of the sergeant in command, were destroyed by fire.[2]

Let us note the date, December, 1678, when La Motte commenced a fort and January, 1679, when La Salle himself started the work on his block-houses on this historic spot.

When La Salle arrived again at Niagara, in August, 1679, his fort was in ashes; his creditors and his enemies had well nigh ruined him. His vessel, the Griffin, however, was ready to sail westward. In the money he hoped to get through trading for furs on her voyage, lay his only immediate hope of financial aid. He abandoned everything else in order not to delay this enterprise. Under such circumstances even his much-cherished plan of a fort at the mouth of the Niagara River was forgotten, for he had neither the heart nor the means to rebuild the burnt block-houses.

For the next few years, Niagara, meaning both the point at the mouth of the river and the store-house at Lewiston, the two being closely connected in the plans of the French for their ownership, often appears in the official correspondence of both France and England, the former being much the more closely identified with the locality.

### DE NONVILLE'S FORT.

In 1685 the Marquis de Nonville became governor of New France. In an official letter from Quebec, dated May 6, 1686, urging the humbling of the Iroquois, he says: " What I should consider most effectual to accomplish this would be the establishment of a right good post at Niagara.

"The manner in which the English have managed with the Iroquois hitherto, when desirous to establish themselves in their neighborhood, has been to make them presents for the purchase of the soil

---

[1] Parkman, La Salle and Discovery of the Great West, page 135, he quotes Letter of La Salle, Margry, vol. II, page 229, and Relation de Tonty, 1684. Margry, vol. I, page 577. Winsor Nar. and Crit. History of Am., vol. IV, page 223.   [2] Parkman, LaSalle and Discovery of the Great West, page 135.   Note.

and the property of the land they wish to occupy. What I see most certain is, whether we act so by them, or have peace or war with them, they will submit with considerable impatience to see a fort at Niagara."[1]

He wanted a "fort sufficiently large to contain a force of four or five hundred men to make war on them; enclosed by a simple ordinary picket fence to place it beyond all insult,"[2] but to this suggestion he received from France no favorable reply.

Early in 1686 Dongan, the English Governor at New York, had also suggested to his government the erection of an English fort at the spot.[3]

During the winter of 1686–7 De Nonville made his preparations to attack the Senecas, partly to punish them for having burnt La Salle's house at Niagara in 1675,[4] and generally because of their unceasing hostility to all French plans. He sent word to the western Indian allies of France and the French troops in the West to meet him at Niagara in July, 1687.

It is not within the scope of our title to treat of that part of this expedition that chastised the Senecas in the Genesee Valley. After that he assembled his French forces and Indian allies at Irondequot Bay, and on July 24, 1687, he embarked for Niagara, reaching there on July 30th; and he at once set his troops to work to build that fort which he had so strongly advocated. The fact that France and England were at peace, and that England claimed the Senecas under her protection, counted for nothing with De Nonville.

He selected for the location of the fort "the angle of the lake on the Seneca side of the river; it is the most beautiful, the most pleasing and the most advantageous site that is on the whole of this lake."[5]

He also states in an official letter, "The post I have fortified at Niagara is not a novelty, since Sieur de La Salle had a house there which is in ruins since a year."[6] So De Nonville's fort must have been on the site of La Salle's block-houses, and it was the first real defensive work erected here.

Baron La Hontan was among the officers of De Nonville's command, and he describes the work as "a fort of pales, with four bastions," and says it "stands on the south side of the Streights of Herrie

[1] Doc. Hist. N. Y., vol. I, p. 127. [2] Doc. Hist. N. Y., vol. I., page 127. [3] Col. Docs. N. Y., vol. III, page 394. [4] Doc. Hist. of N. Y., vol. I., page 150. [5] Doc. Hist. of N. Y., vol. I., page 147. [6] Col Docs. of N. Y., vol. IX., page 349.

Lake, upon a hill, at the foot of which that lake falls into the Lake of Frontenac."[1]

De Nonville, in his report, says: "The inconvenience of this post is that timber is at a distance from it."[2] So the pales had to be cut some ways off, floated to the point and drawn up the steep banks, all involving much labor, and as it took but three days to complete the entire fort it must have been a rather weak affair.[3]

On July 31, 1687, De Nonville, in presence of his army, took formal possession of the fort in the name of the French king, and issued a proclamation, signed by himself and officers, to that effect.[4]

This fort was called after its builder, Fort De Nonville, but the earlier name, Niagara, clung to it. "De Nonville" had no designation of locality attached to it, "Niagara" had, and Fort Niagara it has been ever since. De Nonville started for Quebec on the completion of the fort, leaving a garrison of 100 men, under command of De Troyes, with an eight months' supply of provisions.

Misfortune brooded over the fort from its completion. No sooner had the main body of the French departed, and their Indian allies scattered, than the Senecas, more angered than crippled by De Nonville's crusade against them in the Genesee Valley, appeared before the fort in large numbers and vented their rage on the unhappy garrison. Eight hundred of them laid siege to the place and no Frenchman "dared venture out for hunting, fishing or firewood."[5]

Besides the misery of being thus cooped up in a small fort, and always on the alert for assaults, scurvy set in among the French. The provisions, though plentiful, were of a bad quality; many of the men died. "The fort was first a prison, then a hospital, then a charnel house,"[6] till by spring but 12 men out of the 100 survived.

No sooner did Dongan, the English Governor at New York, hear that De Nonville had built a fort at Niagara than he entered a most vigorous protest against such a step, and demanded its destruction.[7] A long and spirited correspondence between these two representatives of France and England followed, in which the claims of priority of discovery, the ownership of this particular

---

[1] La Hontan, English ed., 1703, vol. I., page 78.  [2] Doc. Hist. N.Y., vol. I., page 148.
[3] Col. Docs. N. Y., vol. IX., page 368.  [4] Doc. Hist. of N. Y., vol. I., page 149.
[5] Parkman, Frontenac, page 166, he quotes De Nonville Memoire, 10th August, 1688.
[6] Parkman, Fontenac, page 166.  [7] Col. Docs. N. Y., vol. III., page 516.

territory, and the allegiance of the Iroquois, particularly the Senecas, were set up by both sides and the claims of each ridiculed by the other.

De Nonville's recent attack on the Senecas made it easy for Dongan to obtain their adherence to his views. De Nonville was extremely anxious for peace with the Iroquois just now, at almost any price. Dongan shrewdly referred some of the points in dispute to a meeting of the Iroquois chieftains,[1] and these warriors declared they would make no peace, nor even a truce, until certain conditions, one of the most prominent of these being the destruction of all the French forts on the lakes, were complied with.[2]

In November, 1687, James II. of England consented to take the Iroquois, or Five Nations, as his subjects,[3] and conferences were opened at London to adjust the many differences between France and England.

While their masters were negotiating, Dongan was materially strengthening his position and his relations with the Iroquois, until De Nonville, fearful of losing both Fort Frontenac and Fort Niagara, decided to abandon Niagara, as demanded by the English and Iroquois, and so expressed his intention to Dongan, as his letter says, "in order to contribute to a permanent peace."[4]

The garrison of 100 men, left by De Nonville at Fort Niagara, July 31, 1687, had been reduced to about a dozen by the end of April, 1688, when a large party of Miamis, allies of the French, arrived, entered the fort, and defended it and the little garrison till a company of French soldiers came to its relief.[5]

On July 6, 1688, De Nonville issued the promised order for the abandonment of Fort Niagara.[6] What a pang it must have cost him! He sacrificed Niagara in the expectation of saving Frontenac. As it turned out he lost that also soon afterwards.

On September 15, 1688, Desbergeres, who on De Troyes' death had succeeded him as commandant of Niagara, assembled his men in the fort, read De Nonville's order to them, and gave directions for obeying it. The palisades were torn down, but the cabins and quarters were left standing, according to the order. "A written memorandum of the condition in which we leave said quarters, which will remain entire to maintain the possession His

[1] Col. Docs. N. Y., vol. III., page 533.  [2] Col. Docs. N. Y., vol. III., 534.  [3] Col. Docs. N. Y., vol. III., page 503.  [4] Col. Docs. N. Y., vol. III., page 556.  [5] Parkman, Frontenac, page 166.  [6] Doc. Hist. N. Y., vol. I., page 168.

Majesty and the French have for a long time had in this Niagara district " was prepared.

In this memorandum it appears there was, first, in the centre of the square a large wooden cross, eighteen feet in height, erected on Good Friday, 1688, solemnly blessed by Rev. Father Millet, on the arms of which in large letters were inscribed:

REGN. VINC. ♡ IMP. CHRS.

(Regnat, Vincit, Imperat Christus—Christ reigneth, conquereth, ruleth.)

Among the buildings mentioned was a cabin for the commander, with a good chimney, a door and windows with fastenings.

Another with two rooms, a chimney, and window in each, etc.

Father Millet's cabin, with chimney, windows and sash.

A cabin opposite the Cross, with a board ceiling.

Still another cabin, a bake-house and an apartment at the end thereof.

A large and extensive frame building, with a double door, three windows, no chimney, floored with planks, and clapboarded outside. No doubt, the chapel.

A large store house, and a well with a cover.

This interesting document will be found in full in Documentary History of New York, volume I., page 168, and in Colonial Documents of New York, volume IX., page 387.

A waiting vessel conveyed the garrison to Fort Frontenac.

So ends one chapter — De Nonville had succeeded in fortifying Niagara, as France desired; but Indian cunning and ferocity, stirred on by English intrigue, and backed by England's demand, had compelled its demolition as England wanted.

## 1688 — 1719.

De Nonville was soon after recalled, and French policy hereafter was more of a cultivation of good will towards the Senecas especially, and the Iroquois generally. Always at variance with the five nations, because of the latter's leaning toward the English, henceforth, in time of peace, France cajoled them, and in time of war awed them by attack.

As for the English, they did not cultivate the Indians' friendship, henceforth, as successfully as did the French.

The regaining of Niagara was one of the main reasons for France's more conciliatory attitude towards the Iroquois, from this time on; and while over 30 years elapsed before she again had a fort there, its possession to her was worth the delay.

It was of more importance to her each year. Her fur trade was being directed to New York, and her possession of Niagara would largely restore it to Quebec. Niagara was the key to the control of the four upper lakes, as well as to the Valley of the Ohio, and it was the most important link in that great chain of fortifications she was building to connect her Canadian domain with that great western territory, which she claimed, and which was called Louisiana.

During the next thirty years, the attention of both France and England was constantly turned to Niagara. Several proposals were made by the respective Governors at Quebec and New York to their Governments for the erection of a fort at Niagara, some of these proposals being made when the two countries were at war, and some while they were at peace.

The peace of Ryswick, 1697, found France in possession of the St. Lawrence and Mississippi valleys, but still without the fort at Niagara. But France was losing no chance to strengthen her position with the Iroquois, who were still friends of England, and, as France ratified a treaty with them in 1701, when England declared war in 1702, the neutrality of the Iroquois was secured and the war confined to New England.

A French plan to seize Niagara was submitted to the Court in 1706, but the alternative and elaborate suggestion of "having recourse to peace and mildness" seems to have better met the royal view.[1]

Article 15 of the peace of Utrecht, 1713, declared the five nations "subject to the dominion of Great Britain;" but as this, literally construed, would have been an acknowledgment that the land on the Niagara was under England's rule, the French diplomats claimed a decided distinction between the "five nations being subject to, and their lands being subject to England." Indeed, it was contended that Niagara was in the Province of New York under this treaty clause,[2] and a protest was made by Clinton against the French trying to occupy it.

In 1716 another recommendation for a fort at Niagara was sent from Quebec to France.[3]

It was through the influence of Chabert Joncaire, a Frenchman, that France was soon to obtain on the Niagara at Lewiston, a foothold which was merely a stepping-stone to the fort at the mouth of the river. This lad, taken a prisoner by the Senecas, his life spared, adopted into the tribe, and marrying a Seneca squaw, obtained great influence with the warriors. In 1700 he entered the French service, and continued therein till his death, forty years after, and this does not seem to have lessened the fondness of the Iroquois for him; for, in 1706, in the "proposal to take possession of Niagara," it is stated "the Iroquois actually suggest to him to establish himself among them, granting him liberty to select on their territory the place most acceptable to himself for the purpose of living there in peace, and even to remove their villages to the neighborhood of his residence, in order to protect him."[4]

In 1718 orders came from France to extend the French trade and to erect magazines therefor.

### JONCAIRE'S CABIN AT LEWISTON.

In the fall of 1719 the French were on very friendly terms with the Senecas, and the time had come to test Joncaire's popularity

[1] Col. Doc. of N. Y., vol. IX., page 773.  [2] Col. Docs. N. Y., vol. IX., page 1061.
[3] Col. Doc. of N. Y., vol. IX., page 874  [4] Col. Doc. N. Y., vol. IX , page 773.

## OLD FORT NIAGARA IN HISTORY. 23

with them, and he was sent to "try the minds of the Senecas, to see if they would consent to the (French) building a house on their land, and to maintain that settlement in case the English would oppose it."[1]

It is more than probable that he was instructed in case the Senecas refused this French request, to take up their old offer to him of a location of a cabin for himself, and to locate it near the foot of the portage. In any event, his influence and his presents obtained the desired consent, and early in 1720 he erected a bark cabin at Lewiston, on the river, hoisted a flag over it and called it "Magazine Royal."[2]

The English at first used every means to have it destroyed, appealing to the Senecas; but Joncaire's influence prevailed against that of Peter Schuyler and Philip Livingston, and it remained.

Joncaire seems promptly to have enlarged it, for it is referred to as a block-house, forty feet long and thirty feet wide, enclosed with palisades, "musket proof, with portholes for firing with small arms," in November, 1720,[3] and Joncaire was its commandant.

Failing to have this house demolished, the English demanded permission to have a similar house at the same place, and this, too, the Senecas refused.[4]

Thus France again secured an entering wedge to the erection of a fort at the mouth of the river. These locations of Lewiston and Fort Niagara, both referred to in the correspondence of these early days as "Niagara," must not be confounded. Lewiston was at the exact foot of the portage, and at the head of navigation on the river, so the excuse of "a store-house" could be made for erecting a defensive work there, that could not be made concerning such a building where Fort Niagara now stands, seven miles away.

Charlevoix, in 1721, visited Joncaire's house, which he calls "a cabin to which they have already given the name of a fort, for they say with reason that in time it will become a veritable fortress."[5] Charlevoix's work was not published till 1744, and in a note on the same page he adds: "The fort has since been built at the mouth of the Niagara River, on the same side and at the exact spot where M. de Nonville had built one."

[1] Col. Docs. N. Y., vol. V., page 588. [2] Col. Docs. N. Y., vol. V., page 588. [3] Col. Doc. N. Y., vol. V., page 577. [4] Charlevoix Histoire de la Nouvelle France, 1744, vol. III., page 227. [5] Charlevoix, Histoire de la Nouvelle France, vol. III., page 225.

A later traveler, at the time a guest of Gov. Simcoe, at Niagara, says of the fort: "It was originally constructed by Mr. de la Tonquiere (Joncaire), three miles nearer the Falls, but was some years afterwards transferred to the spot where it now stands and where Mr. de Nonville threw up an entrenchment."[1]

La Salle's palisaded store-house at Lewiston, built 1679, had no doubt disappeared when Joncaire's cabin was erected.

This fortified trading post of Joncaire's was a most important center for the next five years. It was the headquarters of French influence in this section. A few soldiers were maintained there under the name of "traders," the trade in furs was brisk, the Indians from the north, west and south coming there to barter. The chain of friendship with the Senecas was kept bright by friendly intercourse with their warriors, who constantly came there, French trading vessels often anchored at its rude wharf, bringing merchandise from Frontenac and returning laden with furs.

Thus the English for the first time failed to overcome the French influence with the Senecas and could not succeed in ousting them from their foothold on the Niagara.

In 1721, Gen. Hunter again recommended the erection of an English fort at Niagara[2], supplementing the same suggestions made in 1720 by the authorities of Albany and Governor Burnet.[3]

### STONE FORT AT THE MOUTH OF THE RIVER.

Thus matters progressed in the interest of the French till 1725, when the Marquis De Vaudreuil gave notice that he proposed to build a stone house at Niagara[4], and in the fall of that year Longueil met the deputies of the five several Iroquois Nations at Onontague, and got them to consent to the erection of a stone house at Niagara, the plan of which he designed, and which was to cost 29,295 livres,[5] equal to $5,592. Acting on this consent, he at once sent 100 men to hurry on the work.[6]

The Senecas made no serious opposition to the work, though it is probable it required all Joncaire's influence to induce them to reject the demands which the four other tribes of the five nations, appealed to and instigated by the English at New York, made, first

---
[1] Rochefoucault's Travels, 1799, vol. I., page 257.  [2] Col. Doc. N. Y., vol. V., page 561.
[3] Col. Doc. N. Y., vol. V., page 572 and 579.  [4] Col. Docs. N. Y., vol. IX., page 952
[5] Col. Doc. N. Y., vol. IX., page 953 and 958.  [6] Col. Doc. N. Y., vol. IX., page 958.

for the stoppage and later for the destruction of the structure, although they had previously given them consent, under French influence, to its erection.

This consent of the Iroquois (Senecas) to the French erecting a house at Niagara was ratified July 14, 1726, at a council held at Niagara.[1]

This house, commonly called the "Mess House" or "Castle," begun in 1725, was not fully completed till along in 1726.[2]

Samuel DeVeaux, a resident of Niagara Falls, wrote in 1839:

"It is a traditionary story that the Mess House, which is a very strong building and the largest in the fort, was erected by stratagem. A considerable, though not powerful, body of French troops had arrived at the point. Their force was inferior to the surrounding Indians, of whom they were under some apprehensions. They obtained consent of the Indians to build a wigwam, and induced them, with some of their officers, to engage in an extensive hunt. The materials had been made ready and while the Indians were absent the French built. When the parties returned at night they had advanced so far with the work as to cover their faces and to defend themselves against the savages in case of an attack."[3]

Report says that the stone was brought from Frontenac. DeWitt Clinton wrote in 1810: "Considering the distance and the monstrous mass of stone one would think this impossible. As the stones about the windows are different and more handsome than those which compose the building, the probability is that the former only were brought from Fort Frontenac and that the latter are the common stone of the country."[4] He gave the dimensions of the house as 105 x 47 feet.

Whether openly or by a ruse the French built the first story of the Mess House, the largest and strongest of the buildings ever built on the point of land up to this time, and the Indians, who had promised that the French should not be molested while they were occupied in the work of building the house they had obtained permission for, seem to have kept their word. Thus we come to the first permanent fort at this spot, and a fort has been maintained here continuously ever since.

Joncaire's block-house at Lewiston seems to have been allowed to fall into decay. Early in 1727 Louis XV., King of France, approved

[1] Col. Doc. N. Y., vol. V., page 803.  [2] Doc. Hist. of N. Y., vol. I., page 291.  [3] The Falls of Niagara, 1839, page 119.  [4] Life of DeWitt Clinton, 1849, page 124.

THE "CASTLE" OR "MESS HOUSE," 1896

plans for having it rebuilt that fall, at the same time approving of the location of the house at the mouth of the river, because it would prevent the English from trading on the north shore of Lake Ontario and seizing the Niagara River, which was the passage to the upper countries.[1] Still, as it did not command the portage, he was willing to expend 20,430 livres to repair the house that did.[2]

No doubt his wiser counselors advised differently, for the order was revoked[3] and Joncaire's block house was abandoned in 1728.

That building had done good service; it had given the French the desired foothold on the Niagara River; it had held and fostered the trade in furs; it had established French supremacy in this region, and furnished them with the key to the possession of the Upper Lakes and the Ohio Valley; and last, and most important of all, it had been the means of France obtaining a real fortress at the point where her diplomats and armies had been waiting to erect one for over half a century. It had served its purposes, a fort had been built at the mouth of the river, its usefulness was ended and it was abandoned for ever.

### 1725–1744.

This new French fort, Fort Niagara, from this time on was gradually improved and strengthened, from time to time. Some works of defense must have been constructed at once, for, in September, 1736, an official report says: "Niagara is well fortified. It had only six guns, but Choueguen (Oswego) has furnished 24 of the largest calibre, which are now mounted. People are busy supplying Forts Duquesne, Niagara and Frontenac with provisions."[4]

Still, even the possession of the long coveted fort did not give the French that absolute control of the fur trade that they had expected. From 1727 to 1736 England obtained by far the larger portion of the Indian traffic by means of a liberal sale and distribution of brandy, the "fire water" of the Indians, at the trading post she had built at Oswego in 1722. The French authorities, relying on their advantages of location had made decided efforts to discontinue this liquor traffic, largely, no doubt, through the influence of the priests and missionaries of the Catholic Church, and at Niagara the supply of brandy furnished was very limited.

---

[1] Col. Docs. N Y., vol. IX., page 964. [2] Col. Docs. N. Y., vol. IX , page 965. [3] Col. Docs. N. Y., vol. IX., page 1003. [4] Col. Docs. N. Y., vol. X., page 481.

In October, 1736, an official report by Beauharnois and Hocquart to France, says: "As for the commerce now carried on at Fort Frontenac and Niagara it becomes every year more inconsiderable in comparison to the expenses the king incurs there. These two posts, which produced some years ago as much as 52,000 lbs. of peltries, have these four years past returned only 25,000 to 35,000 lbs. This falling off has occurred merely since the discontinuance of the distribution of brandy to the Indians, whereof it is the king's pleasure that Messrs. de Beauharnois and Hocquart be very sparing. . . . We admit that it is difficult, and perhaps impossible, to sell brandy to the major portion of the Indians without their getting drunk. But it is equally certain that nothing deters them from trading with the French in these posts, and anywhere else in the upper countries, more than the refusal to sell them any of this liquor for which they entertain an inexpressible fondness. They find plenty of it at Choueguen (Oswego), where they repair from 'all the posts of the upper countries without any means of stopping them at Niagara. Sieurs de Beauharnois and Hocquart perceive, unfortunately, no means of destroying or interrupting the commercial relation this drink keeps up between the Indians and the English."[1]

Thus it is clear that as between the obtaining and the not obtaining of drink, the extra travel of over 100 miles made no difference to the Indians of this early date, and the English took full advantage of the commercial benefits thus to be derived over their more conscientious French adversaries.

In 1739, the pickets of the fort were falling down and were repaired.[2]

In 1741, the Governor of New York reported that he held the Five Nations only by presents, and that it would be absolutely necessary to take Fort Niagara.[3]

In 1745, there were 100 men and four cannon at Fort Niagara. Later, the French policy of not selling brandy to the Indians was reversed.

In 1750 Sir William Johnson wrote that a friend of his had seen a letter from the Lord Lieutenant at Quebec to the Commander at Fort Niagara, authorizing him to hold the Indian trade, "even if it cost the Crown 30,000 livres a year, and also to supply them with what rum and brandy they wanted."

[1] Col. Doc. N. Y., vol. IX., page 1049.   [2] Col. Doc. N. Y., vol. IX., page 1068.
[3] Col. Docs. N. Y., vol. VI., page 186.

France saw the growing power of England, and recognized that the great contest for supremacy in North America was near at hand, and tried every conceivable effort to strengthen herself.

In 1751, Fort Niagara was further strengthened.[1]

In 1751, Father Picquet visited the fort. He describes it "as well located for defense, not being commanded from any point, but the rain was washing the soil away by degrees, notwithstanding the vast expense which the king incurred to sustain it."[2]

During the French possession of Fort Niagara, beginning in 1726, and ending in 1759, that fortress served many purposes and yearly increased in importance.

As the most important military post on the lakes, as a standing means of overawing the Indians, as the greatest trading post in the country, and as a center of French influence, it held such a commanding position that England was determined ultimately to own it.

Rumor says, and what circumstantial evidence we have tends to prove it, that during French rule it was also used as a State prison, as were many of the French fortresses, distant from France, in those days.

S. DeVeaux says, "The dungeon of the Mess House, called the black hole, was a strong, dark and dismal place, and in one corner of the room was fixed the apparatus for strangling such unhappy wretches as fell under the displeasure of the despotic rulers of those days. The walls of this dungeon, from top to bottom, had engraved upon them French names and mementoes in that language. That the prisoners were no common persons was clear, as the letters and emblems were chiseled out in good style. In June, 1812, when an attack was momentarily expected upon the fort by a superior British force, a merchant, resident at Fort Niagara, deposited some valuables in this dungeon. He took occasion one night to visit it with a light. He examined the walls and there, among hundreds of French names, he saw his own family name engraved in large letters."[3]

This dungeon is a room 6 by 18 feet in size, and 10 feet high, whose stone walls and arched stone roof contains no aperture for light or air. It is on the first floor, and is to-day perfectly accessible. The well of the castle was located in it.

[1] Winsor, Nar. and Crit. Hist. of Am., vol. V., page 490. [2] Doc. Hist. N. Y., vol. I., page 283. [3] The Falls of Niagara, 1839, page 120.

Deveaux was of French descent, born in the latter part of the 18th century, and during the early years of this century lived at Fort Niagara.

Another statement of his that "this old fort is as much noted for enormity and crime as for any good ever derived from it by the nation in occupation" is probably not far from the truth.

As improvements and extensions were made in the fortifications, Fort Niagara became a place of great strength, and was, and had been for some years when England captured it, the most important spot in North America south of Montreal or west of Albany.

The fortifications at one period are said to have covered a space of nearly eight acres. It was a little city in itself, and the commander was the most important man in, and the practical ruler of, a vast tract of country.

Included within this acreage were the various buildings and fortifications directly connected with the fort proper, and the buildings required for a vast trading post. The gardens, which were maintained by the officers, were located east of the fortifications on the bluff overlooking the lake.

The cemetery, outside the fortifications, was "a few rods from the barrier gate, and filled with the memorials of the mutability of human life." Over the portal of its entrance, in large letters, was the word "Rest," which, if the fort was used as a state prison, must have been full of significance to the unhappy prisoners, at least.

Its location was probably the same as that of the garrison cemetery of to-day, beneath whose sod doubtless lie the bones of many Frenchmen, who, in times of peace and war, "for the good of their country," gave up their lives — some as soldiers in their country's service, others as prisoners of state. Here, too, no doubt, lie the bones of many Englishmen, whose lives ended at this historic fort, far from their native land, but serving her interests.

### 1744 — 1759.

By 1744, the time had come when if England ever expected to own more than the Atlantic slope of the continent she had to arouse herself to greater efforts than mere intriguing with the Indians and sending continual remonstrances to Quebec.

In March of that year war was declared between France and England, and the colonies of New York and New England, in 1745 and

1746, made united efforts to conquer Eastern Canada; yet England failed to aid them to the extent promised, and in 1748 the war was ended by the treaty of Aix la Chapelle.

In 1754, though these two nations were nominally at peace, the frontier was desolated by the Indians at the instigation of the French, and in 1755 four expeditions were planned by the English against French territory — one of these, under Braddock, being for the recovery of the Ohio Valley. Braddock's army was ambushed and routed, and among the spoils captured was his artillery train, which was subsequently taken to, and used in, strengthening Fort Niagara, which was then garrisoned by 500 men.[1]

To another of these expeditions, under Gov. Shirley, of Massachusetts, was assigned the duty of capturing Fort Niagara. Soon after leaving Albany, news of Braddock's defeat was received, and many of the men deserted. The troops were delayed at Oswego for various reasons, till the season was too late, and Shirley led his forces back to Massachusetts.

War between France and England, though it had existed in America for nearly two years, was officially declared in 1756, and in that year another attempt to capture Niagara was planned. Changes in commanders bred internal army troubles, and when the Earl of Loudon finally assumed command, he abandoned the plan that had been formed to attack Niagara.

In 1757, fifty Senecas, headed by one of the principal chiefs of the Five Nations, came to Niagara and held a council with Pouchot, who was earnestly intriguing to detach the said Five Nations from their friendship toward the English.[2]

In 1758, none of the three expeditions sent out by England was directed against Niagara.

In 1759, three more expeditions were sent out by the English, one of them, under Gen. Prideaux, to capture Niagara.

The English reverses of latter years in America had aroused the English Government to the need of a more able management; and under William Pitts' Premiership was commenced the campaign of 1759 that was to retrieve England's honor and losses, and leave her the absolute victor over her great rival on this continent.

The contemplated attack on Fort Niagara, in 1755, under Shirley, had told the French that that fort must be further strengthened, and

[1] Col. Doc. N. Y., vol. X., page 326.   [2] Col. Doc. N. Y., vol. X., page 586.

Pouchot, a captain in the regiment of Bearn, and a competent engineer, was sent to reconstruct it. He reached the fort with a regiment in October, 1755. Houses for these troops were at once constructed in the Canadian manner. These houses consisted of round logs of oak, notched into each other at the corners, and were quickly built. Each had a chimney in the middle, some windows and a plank roof. The chimneys were made by four poles, placed in the form of a truncated pyramid, open from the bottom to a height of three feet on all sides, above which was a kind of basket work, plastered with mud. Rushes, marsh grass or straw rolled in diluted clay were driven in between the logs, and the whole plastered.[1]

The work of strengthening the fort was pushed on all winter, 300 men being in the garrison, and in March, 1756, the artillery taken from Braddock arrived.[2]

By July, 1756, the defenses proposed were nearly completed, and Pouchot left the fort.

Vandreuil stated that he (Pouchot) "had almost entirely superintended the fortifications to their completion, and the fort which was abandoned, and beyond making the smallest resistance is now a place of considerable importance in consequence of the regularity, solidity and utility of its works."[3]

Pouchot was sent back to Niagara, as commandant, with his own regiment, in October, 1756, and remained there for a year. He still further strengthened the fort during this period, and when he left he reported that "Fort Niagara and its buildings were completed and its covered ways stockaded."[4]

On April 30, 1759, he again arrived at Niagara to assume command and "began to work on repairing the fort, to which nothing had been done since he left it. He found the ramparts giving way, the turfing all crumbled off and the escarpment and counter escarpment of the fosses much filled up. He mounted two pieces to keep up appearances in case of a siege.'"[5] A plan of Fort Niagara in 1759, from Pouchot's own work, "Memoires sur la derniére guerre," etc., published in 1781 is given herewith.

From the general laudatory tone of his own work we are led to feel that Pouchot overpraised his own work of fortifying Niagara in

[1] Hough's Pouchot, vol. I., page 53. [2] Col. Docs. N. Y., vol. VII., page 282. [3] Col. Doc. N. Y., vol. X., page 411. [4] Hough's Pouchot, vol. I., page 94. [5] Hough's Pouchot, vol. I., page 142.

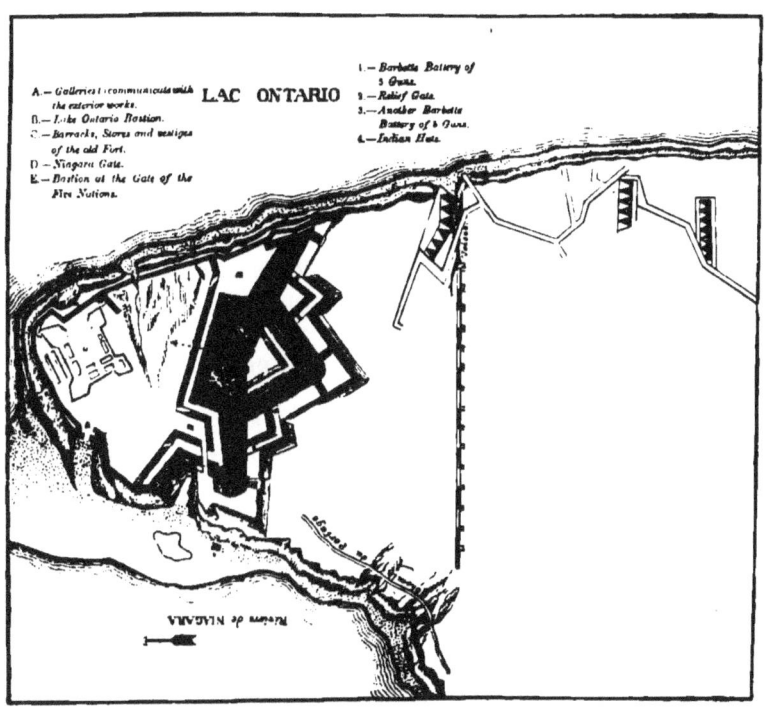

POUCHOT'S PLAN OF FORT NIAGARA, 1759,

With the addition of the three parallels built by the English during the siege. Inside the fortifications is shown the shape and plan of the Old Fort, namely, that built by De Nonville in 1687, whose shape was no doubt retained after 1725, when the French built the castle (which is shown in this cut in dotted lines), and gradually built the fort with bastions around it.

1756 and 1757, when no immediate attack was looked for, otherwise it could hardly have been in so poor a condition eighteen months afterwards (1759, as first quoted), unless, as is very likely, he foresaw defeat when attacked, as he was advised it would be, and wanted to gain special credit for a grand defense under very disadvantageous conditions.

By July Pouchot had finished repairing the ramparts. He gives this description of the defense :

" The batteries of the bastions which were in barbette had not yet been finished. They were built of casks and filled with earth. He had since his arrival constructed some pieces of blindage of oak, fourteen inches square and fifteen feet long, which extended behind the great house on the lake shore, the place most sheltered for a hospital. Along the faces of the powder magazine to cover the wall and serve as casemates, he had built a large storehouse with the pieces secured at the top by a ridge. Here the guns and gunsmiths were placed. We may remark that this kind of work is excellent for field-forts in wooded countries, and they serve very well for barracks and magazines, a bullet could only fall upon an oblique surface and could do little harm, because this structure is very solid." [1]

Pouchot says that the garrison of the fort at this time consisted of 149 regulars, 183 men of colonial companies, 133 militia and 21 cannoniers.

A total of 486 soldiers and 39 employees, of whom 5 were women or children. These served in the infirmary, as did also two ladies, and sewed cartridge bags and made bags for earth.[2]

There were also some Indians in the fort, and the officers may not have been included in this number. The fort was capable of accommodating 1,000 men.

A corvette, called the Iroquoise, fully manned and carrying ten or twelve guns, arrived at Niagara July 6th, and, during the early part of the siege at least, its commander placed himself under Pouchot's orders.

### THE BRITISH BESIEGE THE FORT.

On July 6th an English army, which had been collected at Oswego, under command of Gen. Prideaux, consisting of 2,200 regulars and militia, and 750 Indians under Sir Wm. Johnson, arrived at the Little Swamp, about four miles east of Fort Niagara, and threw up an entrenchment.

[1] Hough's Pouchot, vol. I., page 161.  [2] Hough's Pouchot, vol. I., page 161.

## OLD FORT NIAGARA IN HISTORY.   35

Prideaux had hardly gotten out of sight of Oswego before a force of Canadians and Indians under La Corne arrived there, intending to surprise and capture the place, and cut off the troops from joining in the attack on Niagara. But the French did not make the most of their opportunity for a surprise, and the English threw up breastworks, and on two successive days repulsed the attacks of the French.

Pouchot says of this attack on Oswego, " If all our forces had followed the first detachment, we might have taken these English troops very easily, because they were surprised and much disconcerted at the first moment. Had this body been defeated Niagara would have been saved, as their army could not have received the troops and supplies that were sent for them." [1]

In which view, considering the history of the siege of Fort Niagara, I think Pouchot is entirely wrong.

On the evening of July 6th one of the garrison, who had been out hunting, rushed in and told Pouchot that he had seen an Indian warparty. A reconnoitering force was sent out, which learnt the truth of the hunter's report, by encountering a volley that drove it back to the fort.

Fully satisfied that a siege was about to be begun, Pouchot, while communications were still open, sent a messenger to the French posts in the south-west, calling on their garrisons and the friendly Indians to come to his aid.

In spite of warnings Pouchot seems to have been taken somewhat unawares, or he would have had all needed available troops at Fort Niagara, instead of having to send for them at the very last possible moment.

Pouchot's messenger stopped first at Fort de Portage or little Niagara, a dependency of Fort Niagara, which had been erected by the French at the upper end of the Portage, a mile or more above the Falls, about 1750. This was now commanded by Chabert Joncaire, a younger son of that Joncaire who secured the consent for Fort Niagara's ultimate erection through the Senecas' cession to him for a cabin at Lewiston. Pouchot ordered him to retreat to Chippawa, on the Canada side of the river, and just opposite, if the English appeared, the dependency being in a weak condition. Joncaire removed all the movable property to Chippawa Creek, burned the buildings in

[1] Hough's Pouchot, vol I., page 209

Fort Little Niagara, and hastened to Fort Niagara, where his brother had preceded him.[1]

Prideaux's army consisted of the Forty-fourth and Forty-sixth regiments, the Fourth Battalion of Royal Americans, two battalions of New York troops, a detachment of the Royal Artillery and a large body of Indians, many of whom had till recently been hostile to the English, under Sir William Johnson,[2] whose success in this campaign added to his already great reputation of being the best Indian manager that England ever had on this continent. His name must forever be closely associated with the history of Fort Niagara.

It is impossible in this article to treat of the details of this memorable siege. For these, from the French side, I refer the reader to Pouchot's "Memoires sur la derniere guerre, etc.," published in 1781, a very rare book. Hough's translation, 1866, is obtainable with greater ease.

For the English view I refer him to Mante's History of the late War in North America, 1772. That part of the Journal of Sir William Johnson published by Stone in his life of the Baronet is also an authentic record of events soon after the surrender and as to his dealings with the Indians at that time and later.

On July 8th the English reconnoitered, and on the 9th Prideaux sent a captain of the Royal Americans, Blaine by name, with a letter to Pouchot, demanding his surrender, which was refused; and that night the English, who had already sent a force to occupy the river bank and the roads south of the fort, thus completely hemming Fort Niagara in by land, began opening a trench east of the fort, and on the 11th they erected batteries. Parleys between some Indians in the fort and the Indian chiefs in the English army were held outside the fort, firing on and from the fort being suspended meanwhile.

Several other parleys followed during several successive days, but Sir William Johnson's influence proved strong enough to keep the great majority of his Indian allies from abandoning the English and suddenly becoming neutral, and thus Pouchot's hopes and attempts to detach the large body of Indians from the besiegers proved futile.

The English, working especially at night, slowly but steadily, built three trenches, all east of the fort and each one nearer than the former, the last one being only about one hundred yards from the outworks. They kept adding new batteries, from which showers of

---

[1] Hough's Pouchot, vol. I., page 166.  [2] Hough's Pouchot, vol. I., page 159.

hot shot and shell were poured upon the fort night and day. Those in the fort replied almost continuously, and each morning battered those new works which the English had built during the night. The cannonading on the part of the besiegers, however, was carried on with the most vigor.

On the 17th the English had occupied the west bank of the river at its mouth, and thrown up works and mounted batteries on the then called "Montreal Point," and attacked the fort from that side also. This caused much alarm and danger to those in the fort, and compelled them to erect defenses, as that side of the fort was protected only by an entrenchment.

On the 19th General Prideaux was killed in one of the trenches by the bursting of a shell from a cohorn, before which he was passing. The command of the English forces devolved on Sir William Johnson, who carried on the siege with even greater vigor. The continued firing had on the 22d made a large breach in the walls of the fort, the battery and parapet of the flag bastion being completely demolished, and into this breach grape and musketry were continuously poured in a way that one of the garrison described as terrific.

On the 22d hot shot was poured into the fort from both sides; fires were started by them in several places, but, by great precautions and risk, the fires did no great damage, although many of the fort buildings were of wood.

By the 23d the garrison were in straights. Sacks to be filled with earth and used to repair the damage by shells were all used. There were no cannon wads left, and even hay, used in their place, was not on hand—and the mattrasses on the beds, both the covering and the straw, had been used up. The arms were also in such bad condition, that scarcely one gun in ten was of service.

On the morning of the 23d, under a white flag, four Indians came to the fort. They brought two letters from D'Aubrey and De Lignery, the French commanders at Venango and Presque Isle, in answer to Pouchot's summons for aid—the earlier one saying they were about starting, and the other telling of their arrival at Navy Island, just above Niagara Falls, and asking for information and advice.

Pouchot had sent word that the English besiegers might number 5000, besides 4000 Indians, and the replies said 1600 French and 1200 Indians were coming to his aid.

Pouchot sent four copies of his answer, one by each of the messengers, hoping, as proved to be correct, that one might reach its destination.

On the 29th firing was heard south of the fort and an Indian later brought in word to Pouchot that the French relieving party had been routed. Trembling for the safety of this important post, D'Aubrey and De Lignery had sailed with their forces and coming down the Niagara River (appearing like a floating island, as the river was covered with their bateaux and canoes) had first landed on Navy Island, then crossed the river to Fort Little Niagara, and hurried along the shortest route to Fort Niagara.

Sir William Johnson, apprised of their movements by his Indian scouts, on the 23th, leaving a large force in the trenches, to prevent the garrison of Fort Niagara from co-operating with D'Aubrey, marched south, and, early in the morning of the 24th, met them an eighth of a league from the fort, at a place then called "La Belle Famille," in the present village of Youngstown, in sight of the fort, whose garrison, owing to Johnson's foresight, were prevented from making a sortie, as had been planned, as the relieving force approached. His regulars occupied the road leading from the falls to Fort Niagara, along which the French were advancing, while his Indians were posted on his flanks. The French being thus caught in an ambush, and seeing the English forces lightly entrenched, opened fire on them at short range.

The English Indians poured a galling fire into their ranks, the British regulars charged with great fury, and at the end of half an hour the French broke and fled in confusion. They were pursued for over five miles, one hundred and fifty of them were killed, and ninety-six privates and twenty-seven officers, among them the commanders D'Aubrey and De Lignery, and the famous Marin, were taken prisoners. The Indians of the English force behaved uncommonly well.

Sir William Johnson soon after sent Major Hervey to Pouchot, detailing the above events, and demanding his surrender. Pouchot sent an officer to the English camp, who saw and talked with the prisoners, and returned with the statement that all was true as reported.

An examination of their fortifications, etc., having been made, a conference of the fort officers urged a surrender, and the garrison itself clamored for an end to the siege.

Pouchot had left but 135 men fit and equipped for duty; there were only 140 guns left that were in condition for service; 24 000 pounds of powder had been burnt, and 54,000 pounds were yet left, 109 men had been killed or wounded, 37 were sick, and under the most favorable conditions the fort could not hold out longer than two days, it being in a battered and exposed condition on all sides.

Pouchot assented to a surrender and contended for the best possible terms.

### SURRENDER AND EVACUATION.

These terms stipulated that the garrison should march out with arms and baggage and one cannon, lay down their arms but retain their baggage, be transported in vessels, furnished by the British, to New York, and that they should be protected from attacks by the Indian allies of the English.

These articles were signed on the night of the 24th, and between ten and eleven o'clock on the morning of July 25, 1759, a part of the English forces occupied the fort. Johnson had posted troops on every side of the fort to prevent the Indians from entering it, but an hour after the English troops had entered the Indians scaled it on every side, and in half an hour after more than 500 of them were inside the ramparts, but they remained quiet.

The English had asked Pouchot to have the garrison deliver up their arms under the pretext that they would then be in a better condition to defend the Frenchmen. Pouchot steadily refused, and assured them that if it were done they could not restrain their Indian allies. His judgment was undoubtedly correct, for if, as it turned out, the English could not prevent the Indians from entering the fort, it is not probable that they could have prevented them from assaulting the French had these been unarmed.

Pouchot dined Johnson and some officers, and these officers, after the dinner, helped themselves to all movables in the room.

The Indians took everything they could reach, even to door-hinges; they pillaged the King's store-house, and broke open all the barrels of flour.

The French officers had taken the precaution to put some of their belongings in the powder magazine; these were saved, but everything else was carried off by the victors.

The English officers probably took first pick of everything, the soldiers had the next chance at what was left, then the Indians were allowed to pillage the fort, which they did most thoroughly.

The garrison was drawn up in line of battle on the parade ground, their arms in their hands, their haversacks between their legs. Their officers were with them, and in this position they remained for 30 hours, or until the time for embarkation.

FRENCH MAGAZINE AND BARRACKS.

The Indians at first tried to take the arms from the men as they stood in line. Pouchot had warned his men not to use their weapons against the Indians, but, if attacked by them, to kick them or strike them in the stomach with their fists, for it was of no consequence to an Indian to be struck in this way, nor would other Indians take his part, as they would, were he struck with a sword or a gun. The men obeyed their orders, struggled for and retained their arms.

Had the wind permitted the bateaux in which the English had come from Oswego to be gotten out, it was Pouchot's intention to send a part of the garrison away before giving up possession of the fort, but this proved impossible.

On the afternoon of July 26th, the garrison, with guns on their shoulders, drums beating, and with two cannons at the head of the column, marched out of the fort and down to the beach. Here they laid down their arms, entered the boats that were in readiness, and started for Oswego.

### SIR WILLIAM JOHNSON.

Good diplomat that he was, with such an unruly crowd as his Indians were likely to be, Sir William Johnson seems to have been willing to grant as favorable terms of surrender as he consistently could.

He had established for himself a new line of fame — a military commander. He wanted to have the glory of capturing the great Fort Niagara; he did not want any delay that would enable Prideaux's successor, who proved to be Gen. Gage, to reach the spot and be in command at the surrender. His one aim was to take Fort Niagara. He succeeded; and as the last of the French garrison put off in the bateaux on their journey to New York, he must have stood on the broken ramparts, his mind filled with pleasant thoughts.

He had won for England, and won by his own energy and diplomacy, that spot which she had craved for fully 80 years. Innumerable times had the suggestion for the erection of a fort here by force been made to her by various ones of her colonial officers. Seventy-one years before she had caused France to abandon the fort that that nation had erected here; but for the last 33 years that hated rival had maintained here a center of commercial and military power.

Now all was changed. The English flag floated over the long coveted spot, and the credit of its capture, at the time and for all time, belonged to him — Sir William Johnson.

#### BRITISH CONTROL.

Sir William Johnson's diary gives the number of prisoners in the garrison as 607 men and 11 officers, besides women and children. Of the relieving force which he routed, he captured 27 out of 30 officers, whom he ransomed. Ninety-six prisoners, and 150 scalps, taken in the rout of this relieving force, he divided among the several nations of his Indian allies.[1]

The English losses during the siege, including the action of July 24th against the relieving force, he states as 60 killed and 180 wounded, besides three Indians killed and five wounded.[2]

The ordnance stores captured in the fort were 43 iron cannon of various sizes, 1,500 round shot, 40,000 lbs. musket balls, 500 hand grenades, besides axes, hatchets, picks, shovels, etc., for use in erecting fortifications — also tomahawks, scalping knives, etc.

Let us here note the presence, in the besieging army, of two men, whose names will appear again later on in this narrative.

Joseph Brant, the great Mohawk chieftain, later one of the greatest Indians of history (in some particulars one of the best, in others

[1] Stone's Life of Sir Wm Johnson, vol. II, page 395.  [2] Stone's Life of Sir Wm Johnson, vol. II, page 396.

far from it), was with Sir William Johnson's Indian allies at the siege, then a lad only seventeen years of age.

John Butler, noted later on as commander of Butler's Rangers, father of the notorious Walter Butler, was second in command of the Indians, until Johnson became commander of the army at Prideaux' death, when he succeeded him as leader of the Indian contingent.

After the capture John Butler was a member of the council established at Fort Niagara for the trial of civil cases.

In view of this successful siege, as well as the conquest of Quebec and Ticonderoga in this campaign, it is interesting, and even amusing, to read the criticisms on Pitts' plans for 1759.

"The Niagara expedition was a mistake in the judgment of some military critics, since the troops directed to accomplish it had been used more effectively in Amherst's direct march to Montreal More expedition on that general's part in completing his direct march would have rendered the fall of Niagara a necessity without attack. Perhaps the risk of leaving French forces still west of Niagara, ready for a siege of Fort Pitt, is not sufficiently considered in this view."[1]

Parkman also considers this siege an error.[2]

But Niagara had been captured, to the glory of the British army.

Johnson at once set to work to put Niagara in a defensible condition, and remained there for ten days.

On July 28th, Gen. Prideaux and Col. Johnson of the Provincial troops were buried in the fort chapel with great ceremony, Sir William himself being chief mourner.[3]

This reference to the chapel, and the fact that a priest was among the prisoners taken, shows that the French always paid attention to the spiritual need of their soldiers, though probably not purely for religious reasons; and, further, that the priestly influence in state councils was still powerful.

Johnson made plans, also, for the building, at Niagara, of two vessels, of from 16 to 18 guns each, considering them necessary for the military protection of Fort Niagara and Oswego. He also sent for a number of carpenters to repair Niagara.

In the fort there remained a few French officers and privates, prisoners who were not able, by reason of wounds or sickness, to be

[1] Winsor Narrative and Crit. Hist. of Am., vol. V., page 600. [2] Parkman, Montcalm and Wolfe, vol. II., page 253. [3] Stone's Life of Sir William Johnson, vol. II., page 395. he copies the latter's diary.

moved. Orders were given by Johnson to have all possible care taken of them, not to allow any Indians to have any communication whatever with them, and when they were recovered to have them sent safely to Oswego.

As to the Indians found friendly to the French they were to be civilly treated; inducements to trade, at prices better than the French had given, were to be held out to them; but not more than twenty of them at a time were to be admitted to the fort.

The artillery and stores were to be put in proper order and the artillery placed to the best advantage.

On August 4th Johnson embarked for Oswego, leaving Fort Niagara in charge of Col. Farquhar of the 44th Regiment, with a garrison of 700 men, which was afterwards reduced to a peace-footing of 200.

For several years after the capture of Fort Niagara, Sir William Johnson was — so far as the Indians living within a radius of 300 miles of that fort were concerned — the most important and the most trusted man in America. He had held that position for some time toward all the tribes east of the Senecas, and now that the French were beaten he logically and naturally extended his influence over those who sided with the French, and now looked for favors from the victors.

The real seat of his influence, though he resided much farther east, was at Niagara. There after the capture he had met many warriors and some sachems of recently hostile tribes, and had paved the way for bringing them under English influence and trade. His orders to Col. Farquhar as to his treatment of these Indians were explicit. He was in frequent communication with the officers at Niagara, and it was on his advice and through his personal influence that England extended and maintained her power over the tribes in all directions.

In the fall of 1760, Major Robert Rogers, sent by Gen. Amherst to officially visit several of the former French Posts, arrived, with two companies of his Rangers, in whale boats, at Niagara; and, after a brief visit, taking 80 barrels of provisions from the stores here, proceeded on his way West.[1]

In 1761, Sir William Johnson stayed several days at Niagara on his way to, and also on his return from, Detroit, and busied himself with directions as to the Indian trade, and took pains to walk over and examine his old encampment of 1759.

[1] Journal of Major Robert Rogers.

In 1761, the English re-established a dependency of Fort Niagara at the upper end of the portage above the falls.

Near where Fort Little Niagara, burned in 1759 as noted, had stood, they erected a fortification, and named it Fort Schlosser, after Captain John Joseph Schlosser, who had charge of its erection. He was a German, who had served in the English army at the capture of Fort Niagara.[1]

Shortly before the siege the French had prepared the frame work for a chapel at Fort Niagara. It is uncertain whether it was set up or not, but probably it was. The English, in 1761, took this frame work over the portage to Fort Schlosser, set it up there and used it for a mess house.

In 1762, the English built the present " bake house."

THE BAKE HOUSE.

In 1762, the Indians became dissatisfied, because some of the English traders had commenced building dwelling houses along the portage, which was in violation of existing agreements, and later on in that year the commandant at Fort Niagara was ordered to put a stop to any settlement on the carrying place.

[1] Col. Docs. N. Y., vol. X , page 731.

Fort Niagara was still the spot where, and its commander the man to whom, all Indian grievances were brought, and through him all such disputes were settled, and by him all decisions were enforced.

Such was Fort Niagara when the English first controlled it. It was the head centre of the military life of the entire region, the guardian of the great highway and portage to and from the west; and hereabouts, as the forerunners of a coming civilization and frontier settlement, the traders were securing for themselves the greatest advantages.

To the rude transient population — red hunters, trappers, Indianized bush rangers — starting out from this center, or returning from their journeys of perhaps hundreds of miles to the West; trooping down the portage to the fort, bearing their loads of peltries, and assisted by Indians, who here made a business of carrying packs for hire, Fort Niagara was a business headquarters. There the traders brought their guns and ammunition, their blankets, and cheap jewelry, to be traded for furs; there the Indians purchased, at fabulous prices, the white man's "fire water," and many, yes, numberless, were the broils and conflicts in and around the fort, when the soldiers, under orders, tried to calm or ejected the savage element which so predominated in the life of the garrison.

On February 10, 1763, peace between France and England was formally concluded, and by it France ceded to England all her Canadian possessions.

### THE DEVIL'S HOLE MASSACRE.

In the fall of 1763, Pontiac had organized his great conspiracy, and the Senecas, whose hostility to the English had been noted by Sir William Johnson two years before, and which was partly due to their bitterness at their loss of the business at the portage — Englishmen now monopolizing that business, and employing carts, instead of Indian carriers — were ready to, and did, co-operate with him, urged on thereto, no doubt, by French influence and intrigue, in what they hoped would prove the means of driving the English from Fort Niagara. This hostility of the Senecas had made it necessary to maintain a garrison at the foot as well as at the head of the portage; and for large or valuable trains, guards of soldiers were furnished from the fort.

## OLD FORT NIAGARA IN HISTORY.

On September 14, 1763, a new portage road had been finished between Lewiston and Schlosser, and a train of 25 wagons and 100 horses and oxen, guarded by troops from Fort Niagara, variously stated at from 25 to 300, set out for Schlosser.[1] At the Devil's Hole, the Senecas, to the number of 500, ambushed and pillaged the train, threw the wagons and oxen down the bank, and slew all but three of the escort and drivers. Hearing the firing, the garrison at Lewiston, consisting of two companies, hastened to help their comrades. But the Senecas had prepared an ambush also for this expected action, and all but eight of this force were killed. Some of these eight carried the news to Fort Niagara, whence the commander, with all the soldiers, leaving a sufficient guard for the fort, hastened to the scenes of the slaughter. The Senecas had fled, but over 80 scalped corpses, including those of six officers, bore bloody witness to their hatred of the English.[2]

In November, 1763, these savages still haunted the neighborhood, and killed two of the garrison at the lower end of the portage, as they were cutting wood in sight of their quarters.

Fort Niagara needed to be maintained and well garrisoned.

On the collapse of Pontiac's bold and partly successful scheme, the Senecas, fearful of receiving at the hands of the English the punishment they so richly deserved, sent, in April, 1764, four hundred men to Sir William Johnson at Johnson Hall to beg for peace.[3]

Now was the time for England to make the Senecas pay off the Devil's Hole debt, and Sir William Johnson was the man to force the settlement.

Yet he was too shrewd to think of demanding life for life, or any galling condition that would have involved England in a war for the extermination of the Senecas.

No, he desired most of all that the Senecas should be the friends of the English, and so he made them pay for their past misdeeds in land.

England already had the occupation of this territory along the Niagara River. She wanted also the unquestioned fee. Here was Sir William's chance, and he improved it. He insisted that, beside other conditions, the Senecas should cede to England (as if they had not already deeded it to her three or four times) all the land

---

[1] Holland Land purchase, page 229. Narrative of Mary Jemison, 1826, page 142.
[2] Stone's Life of Sir William Johnson, vol. II., page 208. [3] Stone's Life of Sir Wm. Johnson, vol. II., page 215.

on both sides of the Niagara River from Lake Ontario to Schlosser, thus taking in Fort Niagara and her two dependencies (at Lewiston, which was really only a camp, and at Fort Schlosser) and the portage. The Senecas assented, provided the land be always appropriated to the king's sole use, and provided that a definite treaty be had within three months, and that the lines be run in presence of Sir William Johnson and the Senecas, so as to preclude any subsequent misunderstandings. Eight chiefs signed the agreement, which, by the way, they never intended to keep, although they left three of their chiefs with Johnson as hostages.[1]

### THE GREAT TREATY OF 1764.

Before this visit of the Senecas, arrangements had already been completed by the British to prevent the recurrence of another conspiracy like that of Pontiac. All the tribes whose friendship, with a reasonable expectation of its permanency, could be obtained by presents and good treatment were to be secured in this way.

Against all others, armies were to be sent to crush and overawe them.

The occasion when the above treaty with the Senecas was to be ratified was a general meeting of all Indian tribes who desired peace, at Fort Niagara in July, 1764, to which Johnson had already invited them, in order to readjust their relations with the English Government.

Two military expeditions were planned, one for the West, under General Bradstreet, 1,200 strong, which assembled at Oswego in June, 1764, where it was joined by Sir William Johnson, with 550 Iroquois. They reached Niagara July 3, 1764, and found there such a scene of life and activity as one can hardly conceive of to-day.

In this expedition was Israel Putnam, a lieutenant-colonel of the Connecticut Battalion.[2]

Over one thousand Indians, representing many tribes, extending from Nova Scotia to the head waters of the Mississippi, whose numbers but a few days later were increased to 2,060, were assembled to meet and treat with Johnson.[3]

Such a representative concourse of Indians had never before been seen.

[1] Col. Docs. N. Y., vol. VII., pages 621, 622, 623.   [2] Turner's Holland Purchase, 1849, page 234   [3] Stone's Life of Sir William Johnson, vol. II., page 219

Their wigwams stretched far across the fields and to this picturesque scene were now added the white tents of Bradstreet's men.

Many reasons had induced this great assemblage of Indians. Some came to make peace because the aid expected from the French had not been forthcoming; some because they were tired of war; some because they needed clothing, ammunition, etc., and could get them in no other way; some to protest their friendship for the English; some by an early submission to avert retribution for past offenses; some came as spies, and some, no doubt, because they knew that at such a time "fire water" would be easily obtainable.

Alex. Henry, the trader, tells how the Great Turtle, the Spirit that never lied, on being consulted as to what course the Ojibways should pursue, told them the English soldiers were on the war-path already, and also said, "Sir William Johnson will fill your canoe with presents, with blankets, kettles, guns, gunpowder and shot, and large barrels of rum, such as the stoutest of the Indians will not be able to lift, and every man will return in safety to his family."[1]

The Ojibways accepted Johnson's invitation and were present.

Henry himself came to Niagara at this time, and accompanied Bradstreet westward.

Though this assemblage consisted of peace-desiring savages, their friendly disposition was not certain. Several straggling soldiers were shot at, and great precautions were taken by the English garrison to avert a rupture. "The troops were always on their guard, while the black muzzles of the cannons, thrust from the bastions of the fort, struck a wholesome awe into the savage throng below."[2]

But among all the throng the Senecas were not represented, in spite of their promise to ratify their agreement at this time.

They were at home, considering whether they would keep it, for they had already made an alliance with other tribes against the English. Notice was sent to them, that unless they at once fulfilled their agreement, the army then at Niagara would forthwith march against them and burn their villages. A large body of this war-like tribe, overawed by this menace, at once went to Niagara.

It took all the diplomacy, shrewdness and influence of Sir William Johnson to preserve order and peace among the savages, many who had been hostile to each other, and but lately fighting against the

[1] Henry's Travel, 1809, page 171.  [2] Parkman, Pontiac, vol. II., page 170.

English, and the business of the assemblage detained him at the fort for a month.

The council-room (which was located in the castle) was crowded from morning till evening; but the tiresome formalities which had to be observed on such occasions, the speeches made and the replies thereto, the smoking of pipes, the distribution of presents, the judicious serving out of whiskey, the terms of each treaty, the tax on the memory of remembering what each belt of wampum given by and received from each tribe meant, while fatiguing, were finally successfully brought to an end.

One point of policy was rigidly adhered to. Johnson would hold no general conference; with each tribe he either made a separate treaty, or where satisfactory treaties were already in existence he merely brightened the chain of friendship. By this course he made the best of terms, by promoting a rivalry among the tribes. He also thus discouraged a feeling of union and of a common cause among them.[1]

First of all he met the Senecas, and, till their agreement had been ratified and the lines of the land to be deeded to England had been settled, Sir William would transact no other business.

The Senecas ratified their former agreement, and on August 6th they deeded to the English crown a strip of land four miles wide on each bank of the Niagara River from Lake Erie to Lake Ontario, thus adding to their former agreement all the land from Schlosser to Lake Erie, on both sides of the river. Gen. Bradstreet had asked Johnson to try and get this extra cession, in order that England might have title to the land where Fort Erie, at the source of the Niagara River, on the Canada side, now stands. He was anxious to build a depot for provisions there. Johnson asked for it. The Senecas were ready to do anything asked of them while that English army was on the ground, so they readily assented. They specially excepted from their grant, and gave to Sir William Johnson personally, as a gift, all the islands in the Niagara River, and he promptly gave them to his Sovereign.[2]

This was the first tract of land in the limits of the present Western New York to which the Indian title was absolutely extinguished, and this remarkable land deal, so vast in the amount of territory involved, so beneficial to the whites in the power it gave them

[1] Parkman, Pontiac, vol. II., page 174.  [2] Col. Doc. N. Y., vol. VII., page 647.

for trade, and the settlement of the country, and of such enormous subsequent value in view of very recent developments along this frontier, was closed 132 years ago, within the historic fortifications of Fort Niagara.

From this time on, for fully 30 years, especially during the Revolution, the Senecas were allied with and espoused the cause of the English.

The treaties with the many other tribes were then arranged without difficulties. On August 6th, Sir William Johnson seems to have completed the formalities by having a separate treaty with each tribe with which a new treaty was desired, officially signed.

So fearful was Johnson that some unforeseen occurrence might prevent the successful carrying out of this stupendous negotiation, and so anxious was he about rumors of an attack on Fort Niagara by this savage assemblage, that Gen. Bradstreet's army, now increased to over 2,000 English and Canadians and 1,000 Indians, was detained at Fort Niagara till August 8, 1764.

By that date the Indians, having made their peace and secured their presents, had started for their homes, the great assembly had melted away, the danger of any attack, that the garrison was not strong enough to resist, was past ; and Gen. Bradstreet, leaving an addition to the garrison at Fort Niagara, marched his army to Fort Schlosser, there to embark for the west.[1] The cost of this Indian congress at Niagara was considerable. The expense of provisions, for the Indians only, was £25,000 New York currency, equal to about $10,000, while £38,000 sterling, or $190,000, was expended for the presents made to them.[2] It was money well spent by England.

## 1764 — 1776.

During Sir William Johnson's administration of Indian affairs after 1759, the Common, now the Military Reserve on the Canadian side, was used as an Indian camping ground, and there annually the Six Nations and the Western tribes congregated within gunshot of the fort, to receive their annual gifts and allowances from the British government.

Let us note that when the French built the first stone house at Niagara, in 1725, they did not build it close to the water, either of the

---

[1] Mante, History of Late War in N. A., page 511.  [2] Montresor Journals, N. Y. Hist. Soc , 1881, page 275.

## OLD FORT NIAGARA IN HISTORY. 51

river or the lake. In those days, all through the eighteenth century, and during the first third of this century, a large tract of land, that has now been washed away, existed at the foot of the bluff, extending to the northwest for some thirty rods right out into the lake; and in the memory of men now alive[1] a fruit orchard stood on this land, where now is a depth of ten or twelve feet of water. Quite a strip of land also extended out beyond the present shore line into the river, opposite the castle and above it.

As evidence of this, turn to Pouchot's plan of the fort, on page 33, where this large area is shown as existing in 1759. The French Mess House, or Castle, was originally built, not on the edge of the bluff, but probably one hundred feet from both the lake and river side.

A further evidence of the existence of this, now washed-away land is the fact that on the lake side of the fort, just opposite the angle of the wall, where stand the three poplar trees, plainly visible when the water is low, and generally visible from the wall, though overgrown with water moss, are the perfectly traceable remains of a half-moon battery used in those early days, undoubtedly part of the north demi-bastion, which was re-established in 1789, and used in 1759.[2] The English are said to have added a story to the "Castle."[3]

The first story was built by the French in 1725, as noted before, and the second was probably built by them soon afterwards.

It is not certain, but probable, that the roof of the Castle had been adapted to defensive purposes, and the stone walls carried up beyond the roof, to serve as a breastwork for gunners there. The extra story that the British added to the Castle, was probably the present timbered roof through which so many chimneys protrude.

The two square stone block-houses now standing within the fortifications were built by the French,[4] and the walls carried up beyond the roofs. Sheltered by these walls, batteries were placed on the roofs, and were used as late as the War of 1812. The present roofs on these two block-houses are modern affairs.

The present roof over the old French magazine is also a modern one, being merely a cover over the great stone arch, which is the real roof of the building.

[1] Notably Mr. Thomas Brighton of Youngstown, N. Y. [2] Hough's Pouchot, vol. I., page 168. [3] Turner's Holland Purchase, page 189. [4] Rochefoucault's Travels, 1799, vol. I., page 257.

In 1767 Captain Jonathan Carver, a well-known English traveler, visited the fort, which, he said, "was defended by a considerable garrison."[1]

One of the traditions that has clung to the fort, and that started in the days of English occupation, is, that in the dungeon of the Mess House, before referred to, where there is a well, now boarded over, at midnight could be seen the headless trunk of a French general, clothed in his uniform, sitting on the curbstone of this well and moaning, as if beseeching some one to rescue his body from the bottom of the well, where, after his murder, it had been thrown. This well was subsequently poisoned and its use necessarily discontinued. The well inside the earthworks, and near the sally port, is possibly the well referred to in the list of buildings left by the French when they dismantled the fort in 1688, though I think this is improbable, and that it belongs to a much later period.

From 1767 on till the opening of the war of the Revolution one finds but little public history in connection with the fort, though its importance was in no way diminished, but rather increased.

### DURING THE REVOLUTION.

While the war from 1776-1783 never reached this spot in actual hostilities, Fort Niagara was the spot where heartless Britishers and still more blood-thirsty savages studied, planned and arranged those terrible attacks on defenseless settlers that on so many occasions spread death and devastation through prosperous settlements and regions, and carried off, most frequently to this fort, wretched captives whose term of captivity in the hands of the savages was usually only a living death. The history of Fort Niagara during its entire existence has no blacker nor fouler page, nay none nearly so black nor inhuman, as that which embraces the years 1776–1783.

Far away from the actual seat of war, feeling perfectly safe from attack, its British Commandants seem to have given free scope to every form of Indian warfare that, regardless of its inhumanity, would in any way aid in crushing out the colonists.

During this period portions of several regiments of British Regulars in succession garrisoned the fort. It was necessary for England to maintain it with a strong garrison, in order to impress the savages by show of force, and to keep them continually aroused to the

[1] Carver's Travel, 1781, page 170.

necessity of aiding the English by constant expeditions, organized and sent out from here, of devastation and death.

Sir William Johnson had lost a part of his influence over the Indians during the few years prior to his death, which occurred in 1774.

Had he been alive, I would do his memory the justice to believe that the inhumanities planned at and executed from Fort Niagara, during the Revolution, would never have been allowed, to the extent at least that they attained.

In all his domination over the Indians, and he exercised a one-man power for many, many years, he recognized that a nation, to be thoroughly successful, must not forfeit the public confidence of the world by too great atrocities.

The atrocities perpetrated from Fort Niagara during the Revolution only added to the determination and exertions of the colonists to throw off the British yoke; and the stories of these atrocities gave France an extra excuse to extend the friendly and needed aid that she furnished, at first secretly, afterwards openly, to those who were struggling for their freedom from the rule of her hated rival and her recent conqueror in North America.

On the commencement of hostilities in 1776, a great council of Indian tribes was called to meet at Fort Niagara, and here in September gathered representatives of the Six Nations and ten other tribes, favorable to the English. The assembled chiefs all signed a manifesto in favor of the Crown, and appealed to the Oneidas and Tuscaroras, who were not fully represented, to join them.[1] Some of these afterwards complied. Then, after the customary distribution of presents and "fire-water," the braves were sent back to gather together their tribes for the war-path, to put on the war-paint and to sharpen their tomahawks.

### JOHN BUTLER AND JOSEPH BRANT.

John Butler and Joseph Brant both made Fort Niagara their real headquarters during the Revolution, and, no matter who was in actual command of the fort, these two were the recognized leaders, respectively, of the English and the Indian forces there.

The former recruited from all over the country, but most largely from Western New York and Northern Pennsylvania, the famous band known as Butler Rangers, and their headquarters were at the

[1] Stone's Life of Brant, vol. II., page 4, note.

Fort. Thayendanegea or Brant, the great captain of the Six Nations, gathered his Indians from all sides, and Fort Niagara was their rendezvous.

Each of these two great leaders had many great and good qualities. There was no international code of warfare actually recognized at that time, particularly so far as regarded Indian warfare, and they were, no doubt, influenced to many atrocities by the customs of the age. Many barbarities committed by troops under their immediate commands, were in violation, it is claimed, of their orders and in spite of their influence; while those perpetrated by parties sent off from their commands and outside of the orders given, should not be charged against them. They both repeatedly issued orders for the sparing and protection of women and children, and both on many occasions, by their personal influence, saved many lives. Yet both were regarded as death-dealing and devastating foes, and with good reason.

Walter Butler, a son of John Butler, was also a leader of these expeditions sent out from Fort Niagara to kill, rob and destroy, and in unsavory memory he outranked his more famous father and even Brant.

It should be here noted that just prior to the revolution Brant had led a band of the Mohawks to Lewiston, where he lived in a block house, which stood near what was called Brant's Spring. The huts of his followers were located along the Ridge road, east of Lewiston.[1] A little log building near by was built and used as a chapel, and here the episcopal service was read occasionally by the fort chaplain or traveling ministers. This was probably the first building, outside of Fort Niagara, erected for a church in this section. A good-sized bell, hung in the crotch of a tree near by, called the Mohawks to service. John Bulter, who was superintendent of Indian affairs, lived in a commodious house in Fort Niagara.

On these foraging parties, largely planned by Brant and Butler, during the Revolution, Fort Niagara to a very large extent relied for means of subsistence, and on every raid, from far and near, cattle and supplies were regularly sent back to the fort, their base of operations.

In each and every year, from 1778 to 1782, these foraging parties, and still larger expeditions, were regularly sent out from the fort, and as regularly as provisions were sent back, just as regularly were prisoners and scalps brought back within its walls.

[1] Turner's Holland Purchase, page 265.

The fearful massacre of Wyoming in Pennsylvania in 1778 was planned at and the expedition set out from Fort Niagara. The fatal attack on Cherry Valley in the same year was the result of another expedition sent out from the same fort.

From the commencement of the war, the colonists had endeavored by every means to secure, if not the aid, at least the neutrality of the savages, and, while they kept up their efforts in this direction, by emissaries sent among them, they proved to be futile.

The desire to capture Fort Niagara was continually in the minds of the Colonial leaders, but not till late in 1778, when the atrocities, perpetrated by bands from that far-off stronghold made its reduction seem a matter of necessity, was an expedition planned for its capture.

The Senecas were faithful to the English, and urged incessant war on the Colonial settlements, and in 1779 Gen. Washington sent Gen. Sullivan with a small army to chastise them, even as De Nonville had done eighty-seven years before, and ordered him then to proceed to and capture Fort Niagara.

Sullivan entered the Senecas' territory with 4,000 men, burned their villages, provisions and crops, and defeated them in several small engagements. They fled westward to the protecting guns of Niagara, and Sullivan, for some reason, the ostensible ones being lack of food for his army and lack of boats to transport his troops, gave up the rest and the most important part of his projected expedition, and Fort Niagara was saved.

Had he pushed on, he would have found a horde of nearly 5,000 famished savages around the fort, and a weak and sickly garrison within, and he could have easily captured it. But he lacked the ability to seize the great chance offered him, and Niagara remained in British hands, a scourge to the colonists for three years to come. His expedition merely prepared the way for the famine and want the Senecas soon felt.

The winter of 1779 was very inclement and many of the savages around the fort died from exposure and starvation.[1] In the early spring of 1780 some disposition had to be made of these hundreds of Senecas. They could not be tolerated around the fort and be fed from there, and they refused to go back to their lands from which Gen. Sullivan had driven them. Brant during the winter had strongly urged the Mohawks and the Senecas to emigrate to Canada. The

[1] Turner's Holland Purchase, page 281.

Mohawks and a few from other tribes agreed to this, and went. But the Senecas, under the lead of one of their chiefs, refused, and decided to settle on Buffalo and Tonawanda creeks, where they claimed to own the land through their ancestors' conquest of the Neuters in 1651. They had deeded this to England, as mentioned in 1764, but that nation made no objection. These Senecas and their descendants subsequently became allies of the United States, and fought in our army in the war of 1812.

Some of the Oneidas and Tuscaroras, who had been allies of the English, and had fled to Fort Niagara before Sullivan's advance in 1779 were also about Fort Niagara. In the spring of 1780 part of them returned to their own land and a part settled on a square mile of land some four miles southeast from Fort Niagara, near the Ridge Road, where their descendants to-day reside. This land was given to them by the Senecas. In 1804 the Holland Land Company gave them two square miles more,— these and over 4000 more acres bought for them, constitute the Tuscarora Reservation of to-day.

The Tuscaroras thus became the first permanent settlers in this region, settling here 17 years before the Holland Land Company opened up the territory.[1]

In 1780 and 1781 expeditions were sent out from Fort Niagara with the same deadly purposes and results; notable among them being two expeditions to the Mohawk Valley in 1780, and two others to the same district in 1781, in the last of which Walter Butler was slain.

Opposite Fort Niagara, on the Canada side, each winter Butler's Rangers lived, and at one time six companies of them were quartered there. Outside of and near the fort a few wretched savages built huts each winter and eked out a precarious existence, subsisting on what they could obtain from the scant remains of the garrison's rations. Two sons of Sir William Johnson, Sir John and Guy, both leaders of and agents in the British Indian Department, were prominent during the Revolution, and both were frequently at Fort Niagara during this period.

During the winters of the war-period the garrison of the fort were often on short rations, and the necessity of provisioning it for a long period was frequently represented to the British Ministers, but without any favorable reply.

[1] Turner's Holland Purchase, page 183.

Let us now look at the moral and social life within Fort Niagara during the period of the Revolutionary War.

DeVeaux says, "During the American Revolution it was the headquarters of all that was barbarous, unrelenting and cruel. Here were congregated the leaders and chiefs of those bands of murderers and miscreants that carried death and destruction into the remote American settlement. There civilized Europe revelled with savage America, and ladies of education and refinement mingled in the society of those whose only distinction was to wield the bloody tomahawk and scalping knife. There the squaws of the forest were raised to eminence, and the most unholy unions between them and officers of highest rank smiled upon and countenanced. There in their stronghold, like a nest of vultures, securely for seven years, they sallied forth and preyed upon the distant settlements of the Mohawk and the Susquehanna. It was the depot for their plunder; there they planned their forays," and there they returned to feast until the hour of action came again.[1]

Many men, including especially Butler's Rangers, obtained during their service in the Revolution a training for war that enabled them to render efficient aid to Great Britain against the United States in the war of 1812.

The Revolution ended in victory for the Colonies in 1783. The Canadian side opposite Fort Niagara then became the objective point of many of those colonists who sided with the British during the war, many of whom had here enlisted in Butler's Rangers, and many of them settled there; such settlements having been especially encouraged hereabouts by the British officials during the war.

Among the clauses in the Treaty of Peace at Paris, 1783, was one that provided protection to and time for those colonists who had sided with England, United Empire Loyalists, as they were called, and who were then living in the colonies, in order that they might dispose of their property; and the English commissioners to that treaty, appreciating how unpopular these U. E. Loyalists would be while they remained among their victorious neighbors, and foreseeing that it would be difficult, if not impossible, to get all the separate colonies to ratify such a clause as the American commissioners agreed to, insisted on retaining possession of five western forts, conceded to be an American territory, until such time as the conditions

[1] The Falls of Niagara, 1839, page 119.

named were fulfilled. This also was agreed to by the American commissioners. Fort Niagara was one of these forts. So, in 1783, we entered into what is called in history "the hold-over period," which lasted for 13 years, a much longer time that any of the commissioners on either side had contemplated.

### THE HOLD-OVER PERIOD.

The treaty of peace in 1783 only suspended hostilities, and when soon after Gen. Washington, sent to arrange for the evacuation of the posts still held by the British, he found no such instructions had been given to their commanders. A full consideration of England's real reasons for delay in this matter is not a part of our subject, but it is pretty certain that even till after the war of 1812 England hoped, for one reason and another to be able to hold these forts forever, and ultimately to regain the vast empire she had just surrendered by compulsion to her American colonists.[1]

Gov. Simcoe, formerly colonel of Simcoe's Rangers, a noted British regiment in the Revolution, often and openly expressed this view while holding the high position of Governor of Upper Canada.[2]

As many of the U. E. Loyalists as could do so prepared as speedily as possible to remove to Canada, and the majority of those who went westward, in distinction of those that went to northeast Canada, came by Niagara, and all of them who were in need were fed during their stay here, from the fort.

It is estimated that during 1783 and 1784 no less than 5,000 of the United Empire Loyalists emigrated to Canada, at this point, and this emigration continued up to 1790, by which time fully 10,000 had passed by and received aid at Fort Niagara.

In 1784, John Butler, who was the Indian superintendent at the fort, convened a great Indian council on the Niagara plains, in Canada, opposite the fort, where the Six Nations met the Mississaguas. The commons were covered with their wigwams and the shore was lined with their bark canoes.

The summer of 1788 was an almost rainless one. There were no crops raised, and that year is known as the "Hungry Year." Stores were issued liberally from the fort during 1789 and 1790 to all in need, otherwise many would have starved.

[1] Rochefoucault's Travels, 1799, vol. I., pages 240 and 241. [2] Read's Life and Times of Gov. Simcoe, page 251.

In 1790, H. R. H. the Duke of Kent paid a visit to Fort Niagara and personally interested himself in the distribution of food and clothing to the needy Loyalists.

During the first half of the hold-over period the English kept the strictest surveillance over this whole frontier, and persons traveling hereabouts were more than liable to be arrested and taken to Fort Niagara by the Indians, unless they could exhibit a pass from the commandant, which pass, as the Indians could not read, was a thick piece of card having on it a large wax seal bearing a particular impression.

A trader, stopping at Fort Niagara, called on the commander, who asked where he was going. "To Chippawa," he replied. "Go along and be damned to you," was the answer and verbal passport he received.

A fine specimen of British civility during the "hold-over period."

In the fall of 1789, Gother Mann commanding the Royal Engineers made a report on Fort Niagara. After referring to the re-establishing of the north demi-bastion, which had been greatly damaged and partly washed away by the fury of the lake, he goes on to speak of a survey of the heights on the Canada side of the river about Navy Hall, later Gov. Simcoe's residence, with a view of establishing a permanent fort there, "which might counteract the designs of an enemy in his attack on the Fort of Niagara." In 1790, in another report, he stated "that the space on which Fort Niagara stands is diminishing, from the depredations of the lake" and speaking of the proposed fort said, "it will be about 1600 yards distant from the Fort at Niagara, which, though within the distance of annoying an enemy, could not prevent his carrying on operations against the Fort."[1] Thus we see that Fort George, which was built at a time when England never expected to be obliged to surrender Fort Niagara, was originally designed, not as an opposition to, but as a defense for that fort.

In 1791, Patrick Campbell was here and wrote, "It is a pretty strong stockade fort with regular bastions, palisades, pickets and dry ditches, sufficient against the attack of any irregular army."[2]

By the act of 1791, Upper Canada was formed into a separate government and Col. J. Graves Simcoe was made its first Governor.

---

[1] Read's Life and Times of Gen. Simcoe, page 154.   [2] Travels in North America, 1793, page 169.

He selected the village opposite Fort Niagara as the capital of the province. It had been called West Niagara, as distinguished from the British-controlled fort on the East, Loyal Village, Newark and Butlersburg.

On British soil, yet a border town, his selection of the site was much criticized. But Fort Niagara controlled it, the British controlled Fort Niagara, and he wanted to be near that famous fort, and he then expected England would always retain it.[1]

Here on September 17, 1792, he convened the first Parliament of Upper Canada. It has been claimed, yet not substantiated, that this body met in the fort itself.

However, the garrison took part in the ceremonies, a guard of fifty men from the Twenty-sixth Cameronians from the fort formed part of the military escort, and the guns of the fort fired a salute at the hour of assembling.

The fort was under the Governor's control and his guard of four men at Navy Hall was drawn each day from Fort Niagara's garrison.[2] He had the garrison also as his guard on all occasions. From the fort was fired a royal salute in honor of his Majesty's birthday, June 4, 1793, and no doubt on other similar occasions, and it was as much a British fort during this period as if it had stood on British soil. In 1792 the York, the first Canadian Merchant vessel[3] on Lake Ontario was built just east of Fort Niagara.

In 1793, Gen. Lincoln, Col. Pinckney and W. Randolph, United States Commissioners, arrived at the fort on their way to a great council with the Western Indians, and were handsomely entertained, both at the fort and on the Canadian side, by Gov. Simcoe.

In 1794, the fort was strengthened by the erection of some new works, "especially covered batteries, designed for its protection on the side of the lake and river."[4]

Eleven years had now passed since the Revolution closed, and England yet held the five American forts. This caused much dissatisfaction. Yet the United States neither wanted to, nor could they, afford to, risk another war with the British over their occupation.

So, in Jay's Commercial Treaty of 1794, Article 2, provided, that the British garrisons in all the forts assigned to the United States by the Treaty of Peace of 1783, should be withdrawn by June 1, 1796.

[1] Rochefoucault's Travels, 1799; vol. I., page 229. [2] Rochefoucault's Travels, 1799; vol. I., page 241. [3] Read's Life and Times of Gov. Simcoe, page 271. [4] Rochefoucault's Travels, 1799, vol. I., page 257.

## OLD FORT NIAGARA IN HISTORY. 61

This was a better way at that time of gaining our rights than by war, especially as the United States were not free from blame in carrying out the terms of the Treaty of 1783.

In 1795 the Duke de Liancourt visited this section, and the Governor entertained him on the Canada side; also dining him at the fort, which he told him " he was very loath to visit, since he is sure that he shall be obliged to deliver it up to the Americans."[1]

The garrison consisted then of thirty artillery men and eight companies of the Fifth Regiment. All the breastworks, slopes, etc., were lined with timber. On the land side it had a curtain flanked by two bastions, in each of which a block house has been constructed, mounted with cannon." The Duke adds: "Although this fort, in common with all such small fortified places, cannot long withstand a regular attack, yet the besiegers cannot take it without a considerable loss."[2]

In 1796, in anticipation of their total withdrawal from American soil, the British transferred their patronage over the portage to a similar road built for that purpose on the Canadian side, between Queenston and Chippawa.

Work was also commenced in that year, and rapidly pushed, on a new block-house located up stream diagonally opposite Fort Niagara, on the Canada side, on land that commanded Fort Niagara, being nine feet higher than the roof of the Castle in that fort.

This block-house was designed to receive the British garrison from Fort Niagara[3] and Fort George, an earth fort, was built[4] around it at once.

In less than seventeen years Fort George was destined to exchange an extensive cannonade with Fort Niagara in the War of 1812.

During all this "hold-over period" the British officers at Fort Niagara exercised a certain sort of civil jurisdiction in the neighborhood. From the capture of the fort in 1759 the seat of civil jurisdiction of all this territory was at the fort; and after the evacuation, there being no Federal Courts here, the British officers, of necessity, continued to exercise this jurisdiction, and they exercised it wisely.

At last June 1, 1796, the day set by treaty for the evacuation arrived, but none of the five forts were evacuated. Why? Because

---

[1] Rochefoucault's Travels, 1799, vol. I., page 257.  [2] Rochefoucault's Travels, 1799, vol. I., page 257.  [3] Weld's Travels, 1799, page 306.  [4] Read's Life and Times of Gov. Simcoe, page 268.

the United States were not ready to occupy them, not even Fort Niagara, the most important of the five.

So badly indeed had the United States' army been supplied with provisions that, when notice was sent to the Federal general by the British officers that they had received orders to deliver up their respective posts pursuant to the treaty, and that they were prepared to do so whenever he was ready to take possession of them, an answer was returned that unless the British officers could supply his army with a considerable quantity of provisions on arriving at the lakes, he could not attempt to march for many weeks.[1]

A British statement, but in general substantiated by fact.

The United States Government had sent no soldiers to garrison these forts and had sent no provisions for a garrison. Hence the delay was really at their wish.[2]

### THE EVACUATION.

On August 11th, the order having been duly presented, the British evacuated Fort Niagara and transferred the garrison consisting of fifty men, guns, ammunition, stores, etc., across the river. As the banner of St. George came down from the flag pole at Fort Niagara on that day, the British emblem floated over but one spot on American soil, Millimachinac, which was not surrendered up to the United States until the following October.

So Niagara was the next to the last post evacuated in America.

Gov. Simcoe had arranged to remove the capital of Upper Canada to York, now Toronto, and it was so removed in 1796.

### ISAAC WELD'S VIEWS.

Soon after the evacuation in September, 1796, an English traveler of note, Isaac Weld, Jr., visited Fort Niagara, and wrote:

"Toward the water it is stockaded, and behind the stockade, on the river side, a large mound of earth rises up, at the top of which are embrasures for guns. On the land side it is secured by several batteries and redoubts, and by parallel lines of fascines at the gates and in various parts there are strong block-houses, and facing the lake within the stockade stands a fortified stone house. The fort and outworks occupy about five acres of ground and a garrison of 500 men, and at least from 30 to 60 pieces of ordnance would be necessary to defend it properly. The federal garrison consists, however, of only 50 men, and the whole cannon in the place amounts merely to four small field pieces, planted at the four corners of the fort. . . .

[1] Weld's Travels, page 302. [2] Howard L. Osgood, Rochester, N. Y.

## OLD FORT NIAGARA IN HISTORY. 63

Great additions were made to the works after the fort fell into the hands of the British (1759). . . . Every part of the fort now exhibits a picture of slovenliness and neglect, and the appearance of the soldiers is equally devoid of neatness with that of their quarters."[1]

Later he adds:

" The chief strength of the old fort is on the land side. Towards the water the works are very weak, and the whole might be battered down by a single 12-pounder judiciously planted on the British side of the river."[2]

Referring to the " hold-over period," he says:

"The American prints, until the late treaty of amity was ratified, teemed with the most gross abuse of the British Government, for retaining possession of Fort Niagara and the other military posts on the lakes. After the independence of the States had been acknowledged and peace concluded, it was never taken into consideration that if the British Government had thought proper to have withdrawn its troops from the posts at once immediately after the definite treaty was signed, the works would, in all probability have been destroyed by the Indians, within whose territories they were situated, long before the people of the States could have taken possession of them, for no part of their army was within hundreds of miles of the posts, and the country through which they must have passed in getting to them was a mere wilderness; but if the army had gained the posts the States were in no condition immediately after the war to have kept in them such large bodies of the military as would have been absolutely necessary for their defense whilst at enmity with the Indians, and it is by no means improbable but that the posts might have been soon abandoned. The retention of them therefore to the present day was in fact a circumstance highly beneficial to the interests of the States, notwithstanding that such an outcry was raised against the British on that account, inasmuch as the Americans now find themselves possessed of extensive fortifications on the frontiers in perfect repairs, without having been at the expense of building them or maintaining troops in them for the space of 10 years."[3]

This was also a British view but there was a great deal of justice in it.

On the evacuation of the fort the American public papers paid some nice compliments to the English officers for their friendly attentions, their extensive gardens being left in full bearing.[4] A plan of Fort Niagara made in 1801 shows these gardens extending along the lake front east of the earthworks, so that they then covered that part of the ground where the English dug their parallels and planted their batteries during the siege of 1759, which had not been washed away by the encroachments and the storms of Lake Ontario. The comparatively small matter of leaving the iron shutters on the windows of the castle was overlooked, and these were all taken down and carried to the new British blockhouse.[5]

[1] Weld's Travels, 1799, pages 300 and 301.  [2] Weld's Travels, 1799, page 306.  [3] Weld's Travels, 1799, pages 302 and 303.  [4] Weld's Travels, 1799, pages 302 and 303.  [5] Life of DeWitt Clinton, 1849, page 124.

The British, however, generously left fifty barrels of pork for the use of the new Federal garrison.[1]

The British commandant at the evacuation was Col. Smith, who led the British in the fight at Concord in 1775. It has been said "Col. Smith may with propriety be said to have participated in both the opening and the closing acts of the American Revolution."[2]

## 1796–1812.

The advantages which the Americans, particularly those in any way interested in the carrying trade between the east and west, expected to derive from United States control of Fort Niagara were overestimated.

Soon after the evacuation, in September, 1796, Captain Bruff, the commandant at Fort Niagara, called an assemblage of the sachems and warriors of the six nations at that place, to exchange sentiments of peace, friendship, and mutual aid.

At the close of the Revolution (the "whirlwind" as they called it) these warriors finding they were left by the British under the control of the United States naturally felt alarmed as to what treatment they might expect, as they had been hostile to the colonists—the Thirteen Flames as they called them.

Finding that the conquerors were ready to overlook the past and to treat them with justice, they buried the tomahawk and became good friends and peaceable neighbors of the Americans.

So when the British finally evacuated Fort Niagara, which had been the great headquarters of England's influence so far as the Six Nations were concerned, it was fitting that at that spot the chain of friendship between these savage warriors and the United States should be brightened and vows of continued friendship interchanged.

Among the gifts bestowed on this assemblage, besides provisions, clothing and a barrel of rum, was a large United States flag.[3]

From 1796 to 1812 there is but little public history in connection with the fort.

In 1799, the United States Customs District of Niagara was created by act of Congress. It included the American shores and waters of Lakes Erie and Ontario, west of the Genesee River, and of the Niagara River.

[1] Weld's Travels, 1799, page 302.   [2] Lossing History of War of 1812, page 408.
[3] Turner's Holland Purchase, page 347.

Fort Niagara was the port of entry, and remained so till 1811, when the port was removed to Lewiston.

In 1799, in anticipation of another Indian outbreak, the garrison was reinforced.

In May, 1801, General Wilkinson, who was in command on the frontier, was directed to open a military road between Lake Ontario and Lake Erie, and, at his direction, Major Porter, commandant at Fort Niagara, commenced operations. The road was not completed promptly, for in 1802 the United States mail was still carried from Utica to Fort Niagara via Buffalo and the Canadian side of the river.

In 1804, Tom Moore spent some time with General Brock at Fort George, and doubtless visited Fort Niagara.

In 1805, it became necessary to clear out an old sink attached to the mess house. In it were found the bones of a woman, no doubt the victim of a murder in days gone by.

In 1806, George Heriot, Deputy Postmaster-General of British North America, visited the fort, of which he wrote: "The ramparts are composed of earth and pickets, and contain within them a lofty stone building. The Americans seem to take no measures either for its repair or enlargement, as the waters of the lake make progressive encroachments on the sandy bank, whose summit it occupies, the foundations of the buildings will in a short time be undermined."[1]

In 1810, the commissioners appointed by the State of New York to explore the whole route of the projected Erie and connecting canals made a digression on their journey to visit Fort Niagara.

In De Witt Clinton's journal of the trip he says, "We were received with a national salute and other military honors." Dinner was served in the castle, which, he said, measured 105x47 feet, and was a complete fortification, with prisons, a well and only one door. The fort was in a ruinous condition, the only pleasant thing to the feelings of an American being the new barracks then in course of construction.[2]

Among the troops at the fort during this period was one Carroll, the band leader, said to be a relative of the famous Irish harper of that name, and devoted to music and whiskey. One evening he appeared on parade drunk, and, when reprimanded by the commandant, became so abusive that he was confined in the "black hole" in the castle. Here, in the middle of the night, in answer to his yells, he

[1] Heriot's Travels, pages 149 and 150.   [2] Life of De Witt Clinton, 1849, page 124

was found in a piteous condition of fright, declaring all the hobgoblins and devils in existence had visited him, and begged for a light, a fife, and pen, ink and paper, which were granted him. In the morning he presented to the other musicians the notes of a tune he had composed in the dungeon, and which he called "Carroll's Thoughts on Eternity." He composed at the fort several marches and waltzes, etc., which delighted the garrison and guests on many occasions.

From 1796 till the war of 1812 there was a constant interchange of civilities between the garrison of the Fort Niagara and the inhabitants of the Canadian village opposite, including the garrison of Fort George. Many ties of friendship and, no doubt, of relationship, were severed hereabouts by that war.

When it commenced, there was a yard on the north side of the castle, between it and the pickets, some forty feet wide, and beyond the pickets a space wide enough for two people to walk on abreast.[1]

The fort was then surrounded on three sides with strong pickets of plank, firmly planted in the ground and closely joined together, a heavy gate in front of double plank, closely studded with iron spike. This was enclosed by a fence, with a large gate just on the brow of the hill, called the Barrier Gate.[2] The fourth side was defended by embankments of earth, under which had formerly been barracks. These had been safe, but gloomy, and had been abandoned, and the entrances closed before this date; as they had become infested with rattlesnakes. So numerous had these vipers become in this breeding place, that the soldiers not only did not dare to enter these barracks, but it was impossible to cross the parade ground without meeting them.

## WAR OF 1812.

The official declaration of the war, made June 18th, reached Fort Niagara June 26th, a day after the news had reached the Canadian Frontier by private messengers sent to his agents hereabouts by John Jacob Astor, who had vast commercial interests at stake.

According to the commandant's private admission, the fortifications were out of repair, there was scarcely any arms or ammunition, and only one company of soldiers in the fort, showing great negligence on the part of the War department.

[1] Turner, Holland Purchase, page 191.  [2] Turner, Holland Purchase, page 188.

Work was immediately commenced to repair the picket and earth fortifications, and the well in the mess house was uncovered and cleaned out.

A heavy cannon was drawn into the porch of the castle, new embankments were thrown up and cannon mounted; company after company of militia soon came pouring in from the east and south, raw and undisciplined recruits, gay with any and every sort of uniform and armed with any available weapon.

To make room for these welcome defenders, the officers' families were obliged to vacate their quarters in the fort and were sent away into the country.[1]

Soon there appeared at the fort about a hundred young powerful and active Tuscarora Indians, from their Reservation near by, decorated with war paint and armed with tomahawks and hatchets. Headed by the chief, they had hurried down to offer their assistance to the United States. At this their first opportunity they promptly proved their appreciation of the fair treatment that the newly organized Federal government had extended to their race at the close of the Revolution.

Between the declaration of war and the battle of Queenston regulars and ammunition and ordnance were sent to Fort Niagara.

On August 13, 1812, Gen. Van Renssalaer, who had been appointed to the command of the New York militia, arrived at Fort Niagara, but at once proceeded to and pitched his camp near Lewiston.

It was believed that Gen. Brock, then in command of the British troops along the frontier, contemplated an attack on Fort Niagara and an invasion of the United States, and Gen. Van Renssalaer begged for more troops. At this time there were 300 light artillery and 1000 infantry of the United States army at Fort Niagara.

When Gen. Brock returned to Fort George after the capture of Detroit, many of the American prisoners taken there, accompanied by women and children, were brought to that fort. In September Gen. Van Renssalaer wrote to Gen. Brock relative to their condition, to the end that they might be relieved from Fort Niagara, and offering to receive the women and children at that fort, and by order of Gen. Brock these women and children were landed at Fort Niagara.[2]

[1] Turner's Holland Purchase, page 190.  [2] Tupper's Life of Sir Isaac Brock, 1845, page 297.

Responding to Gen. Dearborn's insistance that Upper Canada should be conquered before winter, Gen. Van Renssalaer planned the capture of Queenston Heights, opposite Lewiston, and preparations were made for the attack on October 13th. The flying artillery

THE SOUTHWEST BLOCK HOUSE.

under Lieut.-Col. Fenwick, as well as most of the garrison at Fort Niagara, were sent to Lewiston. It is not necessary to our subject to discuss the details of this battle.

Gen. Brock was at Fort George expecting an attack, but under the belief that it would be made from Fort Niagara. Hearing the cannonading he hastened to Queenston, only to see the heights carried by the Americans under Lieut. Wool. He at once sent word to Fort George for reinforcements and also an order for an immediate bombardment of Fort Niagara.

His instructions were obeyed and Fort Niagara was again under fire. The south block-house in this fort promptly replied and occasionally turned its guns on the Canadian village of Newark, where, by reason of

## OLD FORT NIAGARA IN HISTORY. 69

the hot shot used (for there was a furnace in Fort Niagara specially built for heating cannon balls), many of the buildings were set on fire.

The cannonading lasted for several hours; shells also were thrown from Fort George, and from these the men in Fort Niagara had no protection. This fact, and the bursting of a cannon decided Capt. Leonard, who was in command, to abandon Fort Niagara, and with the small garrison of about twenty men he started for Lewiston, leaving the fort empty. He had proceeded but a short distance when he saw the British putting off in boats from near Fort George to occupy it. Reconsidering his action, he hurried his men back into it and

THE NORTHEAST BLOCK HOUSE.

held it unmolested till the regulars returned very early the next morning from Queenston.

In rallying his forces to recapture Queenston Heights Gen. Brock was killed. Had he learnt that Fort Niagara was poorly garrisoned he was too good a soldier not to have ordered its attack, and why Major Evans, who was in command of Fort George, plainly seeing the small number of men in the garrison, and Leonard's cowardice, as evinced by his retreat, did not promptly storm it, for it would have been captured with ease, is unexplained.

After the battle of Queenston, many of the wounded Americans were conveyed to Fort Niagara and lodged in any available place, even the cellars of the castle being converted into a hospital.

The British army after its success at Queenston marched back to Fort George — at once a column of victory and a funeral train, for it carried the body of its late commander.

Gen. Brock was buried in a cavalier bastion at Fort George on October 16th. Col. Scott, who had been captured at Queenston, was then a prisoner at Newark, and at his suggestion, Gen. Van Renssalaer issued orders that immediately after the funeral was over minute guns should be fired from Fort Niagara, "as a mark of respect due to a brave enemy." [1]

Early in the morning of November 21st hostilities were renewed. The British had prepared mortars and planted a long train of battering cannon behind breast-works on the margin of the river, under Fort George. Five of these batteries and the guns of Fort George bombarded Fort Niagara from sunrise to sunset.

The garrison of that fort had been reinforced after the 13th of October by the 13th Regiment of U. S. troops, but was not yet supplied with a sufficient quantity of artillery or ammunition. Col. George McFeeley was in command. During November 21st, 2,000 cannon balls and 180 shells were discharged against Fort Niagara.

The shells did little harm, but many of the cannon balls, having been heated, set fire to several buildings in and about the fort. Thanks to the ceaseless efforts of the garrison, none of the buildings were burnt. Fort Niagara returned the fire of the British with alacrity and vigor. A six-pounder had been mounted on top of the mess house, a twelve-pounder on the southwest block-house, other cannon on the north block-house. There was an eighteen-pounder in the southeast battery, and an eighteen and also a four-pounder on the west battery. The Salt Battery, a dependency in the present village of Youngstown, mounting an eighteen and a four-pounder, also did effective work, and, when their gun wadding gave out during the worst of the bombardment, the officers and men tore up their flannel waist coats, shirts and trousers to supply their guns. Several houses in

[1] Tupper's Life of Sir Isaac Brock, 1845, page 333.

Newark were set on fire by hot shot during this bombardment, but were saved. The mess house at Fort George and some buildings near it, however, were set on fire by hot shot and were burned.

An instance of female bravery at Fort Niagara on this day must also be chronicled. A private in the U. S. Artillery, Doyle by name, who had been stationed at the fort, was among the prisoners taken at Queenston. His wife had remained in the fort and, resenting the refusal of the British to parole her husband, she insisted on filling his place and doing his duty against the enemy. She accordingly, during the bombardment, attended the six-pounder on the Mess house, served it with hot shot, regardless of the shells which were falling around her, and never quitting her post till the last gun had been discharged.

The bombardment effected nothing of great moment on either side of the river. Buildings in both forts were set on fire and the works of both were damaged. American marksmanship silenced one of the Canadian batteries for a time. The loss of life, fortunately, was small on both sides, two being killed and seven wounded on the American side, and more on the British side.[1]

During the winter of 1812-13 there were no events of note at the fort. It was fully garrisoned, for it was by no means improbable that the British might, at any time, attempt its capture, and more than one of the officers at Fort George across the river formed plans for its assault, each hoping thereby to win for himself military fame; but none of these plans were ever attempted. Early in 1813, Col. Scott, who was among the prisoners exchanged, arrived at Fort Niagara.

At the breaking out of the war the Mohawk Indians had sided with the British, but the Senecas, located near Buffalo, had promised not to engage in the war, unless on the side of the United States.

When the British took possession of Grand Island, which the Senecas claimed as their territory, which claim the State of New York had recognized, the young Seneca braves could no longer be restrained, and they made a declaration of war in writing, said to be the first instance of its kind in Indian history. The United States had been reluctant to employ savages, but the action of the British in securing the aid of the Mohawks, caused Gen. Lewis, who commanded Fort Niagara in 1813, to invite the Senecas to the fort and to seek their aid.

[1] Official Report of Col. McFeeley's The War, page 109.

Three or four hundred Senecas in their war paint came, but on learning that they were expected to exert rather a moral influence than to use the tomahawk they went away in disgust.

Their friendly attitude, and later on their active service along the frontier, however, were of great benefit to the Americans.

On April 27th the Americans captured Little York (Toronto), and the tremendous explosion of the powder magazine there was plainly heard at Fort Niagara.

On May 8th Commodore Chauncey's fleet brought Gen. Dearborn and his victorious army from York to Four-mile Creek, east of Fort Niagara, where they landed. As many as possible were quartered in Fort Niagara — every available room being occupied and the parade ground being covered with their tents. The balance encamped at Four-mile Creek. All of the wounded were also brought over and cared for at the camp or in houses in the neighborhood.

### CAPTURE OF FORT GEORGE.

Gen. Dearborn established his headquarters in Fort Niagara, Col. Scott being his adjutant; and plans were at once made to capture Fort George. Being confined to his bed by sickness, Gen. Dearborn's orders were issued from his sick room.

On May 26th, a number of boats which the Americans had built at the "meadows," five miles up stream from Fort Niagara, were launched. The British battery opposite opened fire on them, and as they came down stream the batteries and Fort George cannonaded them. Fort Niagara, its batteries and dependencies replied vigorously.

When night came the boats were safely taken past Fort George, and around Fort Niagara to the lake shore, to Four-mile Creek.

Early on the morning of May 27th the troops were embarked from the fort and the camp on the vessels and boats, and at once proceeded to the attack.

The guns of Fort Niagara and its batteries were turned on Fort George. The warships took their assigned positions, some to bombard Fort George and its batteries, some to silence the batteries on the lake near where the troops were to land.

Amidst a terrific bombardment, the men led by Col. Scott, landed, drove back the British, captured Fort George, and by noon were in quiet possession of every battery on the river, the British fleeing with precipitation.

## OLD FORT NIAGARA IN HISTORY. 73

A storm coming up, the fleet sailed up the river and anchored nearly opposite Fort George.

From May 27th till December, 1813, Fort George was in the possession of the Americans, and the headquarters of the Army of the Center was here, and thus on British soil. General Dearborn, General Wilkinson, Colonel Scott, General Harrison and General McClure of the New York Militia were successively in command, and were frequently at Fort Niagara.

### FORT GEORGE ABANDONED.

On December 10th, word came to Fort George that 1,500 British regulars and 700 Indians were advancing toward it, with a view to its capture and the expulsion of the Americans from Canadian soil hereabouts.

McClure's garrison was not a large one; only sixty effective men. He was not a man of courage. He decided to abandon Fort George and to concentrate all his troops in Fort Niagara.

For about two months he had had in his possession the following, sent from Sackett's Harbor:

WAR DEPARTMENT, October 4, 1813.

Sir,—Understanding that the defense of the post committed to your charge may render it proper to destroy the town of Newark, you are hereby directed to apprise the inhabitants of this circumstance, and invite them to remove themselves and their effects to some place of greater safety.

JOHN ARMSTRONG.

Brigadier-General MCCLURE, or officer commanding at Fort George.

McClure had never carried out this order. All of a sudden, in the middle of a most rigorous winter, he decided to abandon Fort George. Most of the guns were spiked, and all movable stores put on boats. Then, falling back on this old order from the war department (which had been sent to him long before winter set in, and with the very idea of preventing unnecessary hardship), he gave notice to the inhabitants of Newark that in a few hours the town would be burnt. This order of his own he carried out. The village was set on fire in several places, and 150 houses were consumed. While it was burning the American troops crossed to Fort Niagara.

It was a sorry day for that fort (and for the frontier) when it became the headquarters of Gen. McClure.

In such haste was he to get away from the rapidly advancing British troops, and to get behind the guns of Fort Niagara, that he did not even try and demolish any of the works of Fort George; and his excuse for the burning of Newark, "that it might not be left as a shelter for the enemy," was nullified by the fact that he left the barracks on the river bank intact, and serviceable tents for 1500 men in Fort George.[1] Several good cannons and a quantity of shot were also left behind.

When the British took possession of Fort George and the ruins of Newark it was toward Fort Niagara, behind whose walls McClure, the destroyer of Newark, had taken refuge, that their thoughts at once turned for revenge.

Gen. McClure, possibly appreciating this, promptly, on December 12th, moved his headquarters to Buffalo, from whence, on December 18th, he issued a proclamation warning the people of the preparations of the British to make a descent on the American side of the Niagara.[2]

But he made no provision against it, not even sending a special message to the officers in Fort Niagara, trusting solely to his general order to them of some days before.[3]

Capt. Leonard had been left in command of that fort, and warned that an attack might be expected. It was this same officer, I believe, who a little over a year before had evacuated this same fort; but, on seeing the British starting to occupy it, had plucked up courage to return and hold it.

Whether he was a traitor, as was strongly suspected, but not conclusively proven, or merely without courage, military ability and foresight, like too many of the American officers who held commissions on this frontier during the War of 1812, his negligence was criminal.

### FORT NIAGARA CAPTURED.

On their arrival, as they stood gazing on the ruins of Newark, Colonel Murray said to General Drummond, "Let us retaliate by fire and sword." "Do so," replied that commander, "swiftly and thoroughly."

[1] British Official Report, Niles Register, vol. V., No. 21. [2] McClure's Proclamation, December 18, 1813. [3] McClure's General Order, December 12, 1813.

## OLD FORT NIAGARA IN HISTORY. 75

So intense was the feeling of the Britishers that preparations were rapidly made. On the night of December 18th, a cold, dark, night, Colonel Murray crossed the river at the "Meadows," five miles above Fort Niagara, with one thousand men, British and Indians. Carrying axes, scaling ladders and other implements for assault, shielded by the darkness, they pressed on to Fort Niagara. The advance pickets of the Americans were captured in silence, and the force placed for a simultaneous attack at several points — five companies of the 100th Regiment were to assail the main gate, three companies of the same regiment were to storm the eastern semi-bastion, the Royal Scots Grenadiers were to assault the salient angle of the works, and the Forty-first Regiment was to support the principal attack.[1]

These preparations were unnecessary. At four o'clock in the morning of Sunday, December 19th, when the assailants reached the main gate of the fort, they found it wide open and unguarded. They rushed in and seized the sentinels, who, in fright, gave up the countersign. There were about 400 men in the garrison, some of them in the hospital; but enough, had the fort been properly patrolled and the most ordinary precautions been taken against a sudden attack, to have defended it. But the evening before, Leonard, their commander, without notice to his officers or instructions to them, had quietly slipped away to his home, which was at the meadows, where the assailants landed.

The occupants of the southwest block-house and the invalids in the red barracks jumped from their beds on hearing the noise, and made a determined stand, killing half a dozen, and wounding more, of the assailing party.

This resistance was overcome, and the fort was in possession of the British before the rest of the garrison were fully awake. Few shots were fired; the bayonet was the weapon[2] and revenge the watchword. Little if any attempt was made to curb the British soldiers' thirst for blood, and many of the garrison, especially hospital patients, were bayoneted after all resistance had ceased.

The loss of the Americans was 80 killed, 14 wounded (these figures tell the story of British revenge), and 244 made prisoners; and only about 20 escaped.

Col. Murray was wounded early in the attack, and resigned the command to Col. Hamilton, "under whose superintendence, it is stated,

---
[1] Lossing's History of War of 1812, page 633, he quotes Colonel Murray's official report.
[2] Gen. Drummond's Official Report, December 19, 1813.

the women of the garrison were stripped of their clothing and many of them killed, and the persons of the dead officers treated with shocking indignity."[1]

The spoils of war, captured in the fort, consisted of 27 cannon, 3,000 stands of arms and many rifles, a large amount of ammunition and commissary stores, clothing and camp equipage of every description.

### DEVASTATION OF THE FRONTIER.

When in full control of the fort, the British fired one of the largest cannon as a signal of victory, and Gen. Riall, who, with his bloodthirsty soldiers and Indians, was waiting at Queenston for the news, at once crossed his forces to Lewiston, there to commence the devastation of the frontier.

Thus inside of 10 days the control of both Fort Niagara and Fort George, which included the control of the river, passed, amid scenes of slaughter and devastation, from American to British hands, and once more the flag of England floated over the ramparts of Fort Niagara.

Bloody as was the vengeance wreaked on the surprised garrison, it was not so bad as that inflicted by the British troops and their Indian allies, the latter led by British officers in war paint, on the defenseless inhabitants living between Fort Niagara and Tonawanda. Almost every house in that territory and all movable property was burnt, and men, women, children and even babes were slain and scalped.

Marauding parties from Fort Niagara were sent out and burnt all buildings to the eastward for a distance of 18 miles.

Gen. McClure blamed Capt. Leonard for the loss of the fort, charging him with gross neglect. Leonard, within a few days, gave himself up to the enemy, retiring with his family to Canada.[1] Later he returned and surrendered himself. He was tried by court-martial and dismissed from the army.

The British held undisputed possession of the fort from its capture until the close of the war.

Its occupation was of no direct benefit to England. The entire American Frontier was desolate and in ruins. The rest of the war so far as this section was concerned, was carried on on Canadian soil; and the rumored and expected attacks, to be made from Fort Niagara on the settlement at Batavia and elsewhere, never occurred.

[1] J. L. Thompson, History of the War, 1816, page 186. [1] Fay's Official Reports, page 167.

On March 27, 1815, under article 1 of the Treaty of Ghent, the fort was surrendered to and occupied by the United States, and its flag has floated over it ever since.

On August 8, 1817, James Monroe, President of the United States, paid a brief visit to the fort.

In the summer of 1825 the Marquis de Lafayette, the guest of the nation, paid a visit to Fort Niagara. Major Thomson, at the head of his officers, met him outside the fort, and as he entered the gate a salute of 24 guns was fired. He dined at the fort, which he was told had been much repaired since the war of 1812, so that no traces of the damage then done remained.[1]

### OPENING OF THE ERIE CANAL.

As already noted, all British goods shipped to the West had been carried over the Canadian portage since 1796; but the great highway for American commerce to and from the rapidly settling West was from Oswego to Lewiston, to Schlosser, and Buffalo; and as the vessels rounded the point where Fort Niagara stood it gave their crews a feeling of pride, and a sense of security, to see on every trip the national flag floating over a national fort, garrisoned by national troops.

But the fall of 1825 brought the completion and official opening of the Erie Canal, and the large commerce which had passed this way took the new route. The increase of a population, which had been largely dependent on the business of the portage, was stopped, and Buffalo, the terminus of the Erie Canal, rapidly increased at the expense of the territory on the lower Niagara.

Thus another reason why Fort Niagara should be maintained as a defensive work, namely, the protection of an important inland, and yet a frontier commerce, which passed under its guns, was removed.

The projection of the Welland Canal, which was completed in 1829, took away another though a directly opposite reason for Fort Niagara's maintenance. Canadian commerce, on taking this new and abandoning the Niagara way westward, could no longer, in the event of war, be harassed by Fort Niagara's guns.

So in May, 1826, the troops were withdrawn and the historic fort in its entirety left in charge of one man.

[1] Lafayette in America, 1829, vol. II., page 213

## ANTI-MASONIC AGITATION.

In September, 1826, Fort Niagara was called to the attention of the nation and the civilized world, even more prominently than it had ever been in all its history, by the Anti-Masonic movement. William Morgan, a resident of Batavia, and a Free Mason, had threatened to divulge the secrets of that body in print. It is generally credited that members of that order, failing to get control of Morgan's manuscript revelations, had him arrested on some petty charge and jailed at Canandaigua. On being liberated he was thrust into a closed carriage

WILLIAM MORGAN.

in waiting and, always accompanied by three men, with relays of horses, taken through Rochester, along the Ridge Road to Lewiston, and thence to Fort Niagara, where the driver was told to stop near the graveyard. Here the four men got out, the carriage was sent away, and the party proceeded to the water's edge, got into a boat and crossed to Canada, whence, after a two hours' absence, they returned, and entered the fort. This was after midnight, September 13, 1826. Preparations had been completed at Fort Niagara for the reception of the kidnapped man. He was at once placed in confinement, but tradition differs as to where he was confined. The old French magazine, the dark cell in the "castle," and the respective dark cells in the two block-houses, being all pointed out as the location. A big iron key, nearly eleven inches in length, kept in the office of the Quartermaster, is shown as the key of "Morgan's dungeon," but it throws no light as to that dungeon's location. The magazine seems to be the probable location. On September 14th a steam boat, conveying a number of Masons to a meeting at Lewiston, stopped at the fort's wharf, and several of those on board went into the fort and saw Morgan; others of the party refused to enter it. On the same day it was reported at Lewiston "that there was trouble at the fort." Morgan remained in confinement for six days, often visited by Masons, none others being allowed to see him. He was quite "noisy" at first, and his visitors tried to "quiet" him. He refused to give up his manuscript, or to tell where it could be found. He begged to see his wife and children, and is reported to have said several times that he would rather stay in the magazine than be bled to death by the doctor. He made ineffectual attempts to break through the heavy doors of the building.

Frequent consultations were held as to what disposition was to be made of him. One plan was to settle him on a farm in Canada; another, to hand him over to a Masonic commander of some British war ship; and another, to drown him in the lake. Masons who admitted having participated in these consultations said they strenuously opposed the last, even to a point of quarreling with their comrades.

William Morgan was last heard of in confinement in the fort on September 19, 1826. He disappeared, and all trace of him was absolutely lost.

A tremendous excitement, of course, followed his disappearance. Popular tradition said he was taken blindfolded by masked men from the fort, forced into a boat, which was rowed out into the lake, and that he was dropped overboard, heavy weights being attached to his body.

Investigating committees were appointed everywhere, and Fort Niagara thoroughly examined by many of them. The bed of the Niagara River near the fort and far out into the lake was dredged for weeks, but without result.

A little more than a year afterwards a body was found on the lake shore over twenty miles east of Fort Niagara. A coroner's jury said "unknown," but the anti-Masons thought it was Morgan; had it exhumed, proved its identification as Morgan and had it removed to Batavia and buried. It was "a good enough Morgan for them till after election." Additional information having subsequently been obtained, another inquest was held, and it was proved to be the body of one Timothy Monroe.

Several men, including the Sheriff of Niagara County, the Keeper of Fort Niagara, and several citizens of the neighborhood, were arrested and long afterwards tried. No proof of Morgan's death could be produced. None of those sworn at the trials for his abduction were at the magazine when Morgan left it, nor could they learn his fate. Some witnesses refused to testify, three men plead guilty, and one was convicted of complicity in Morgan's abduction. The Sheriff of Niagara County was removed from office.

Thus, within the historic walls of old Fort Niagara, where William Morgan was last seen alive, occurred the birth of the Anti-Masonic party, which, for years afterward, in New York and several other states, exercised such a great political influence.

Fort Niagara at this time was a desolate place, without a garrison. The only house near it was a small ferry house, occupied by the man who had charge of the fort.

No matter what their intentions in regard to him were, it was just exactly the kind of a place for Morgan's abductors to confine him in while they were deliberating as to what should be their final step in their unlawful course;—being a lonely, uninhabited spot, whose owner in those days of slow communication could not interfere with their proceedings; located a mile away from any human habitation, on this side of the river, and out of the jurisdiction of the people across the river.

### MODERN FORT NIAGARA.

Since 1826 Fort Niagara has not been considered as a really defensive work. Indeed, in the early part of that year it was considered of so little importance that, as already noted, the garrison was withdrawn, and for about ten years it remained an abandoned and deserted post. About 1836 it was re-occupied and garrisoned, and has been occupied without interruption ever since.

In old days in the first story of the Castle was the large mess room, used also as an assembly room on all occasions, a large spacious apartment from whose windows one looked out on the broad waters of Lake Ontario. This famous apartment, wherein the French and English commandants at the fort, as representatives of their respective sovereigns, met and treated with the various sachems of the Indian tribes—wherein were held military and commercial councils and social gatherings—has long, long ago been partitioned off into several small rooms. Somewhere within the fort, in an unmarked and unknown grave, rest the remains of General Prideaux, to whom Pitt entrusted the responsible duty of capturing the fort in 1759.

Somewhere also within the ramparts tradition says sums of gold and silver, buried at various times and for various reasons, lie concealed. Many applications have been made for permission to dig for and unearth these treasures, but all have been refused.

In 1839 the stone wall towards the river was constructed.

The "Patriot War" in 1837 came very near involving this country in another war with England along this frontier; in which case Fort Niagara would again have been brought into prominence. But England's apology for the Caroline episode prevented such a thing.

In 1861 the present brick walls were constructed, outside the line of the old earthworks.

In 1865 a lighthouse was established here, the light being placed on top of the "castle."

In 1873 the present comely lighthouse was erected.

The entire post has been rebuilt, a few buildings at a time, officers' quarters, barracks, hospital, etc., within the past twenty years, all located south of the "old" fort, leaving that as a hallowed memory of the past.

In 1880, the present rifle range was constructed, and is used annually by the Department of the East.

In 1893, a life saving station was established here.

The land embraced in the fort reserve amounts to 288 acres, and is in latitude 43° 15' N., longitude 2° west from Washington.

And so we come down now to the Centennial of the evacuation of the "old" fort by the British in 1796.

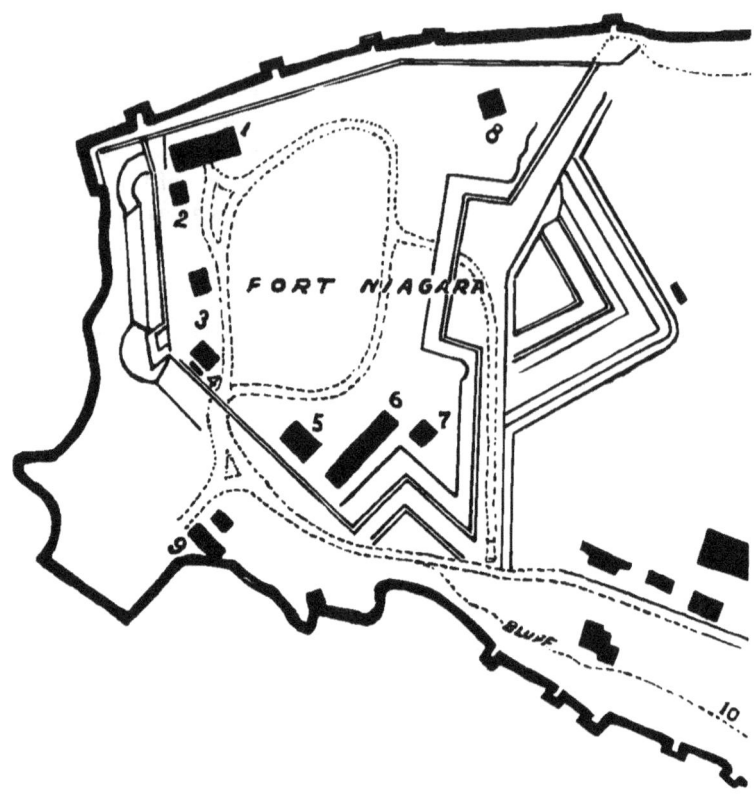

PLAN OF OLD FORT NIAGARA, 1896.

1. The Castle, or Mess House; commenced 1725.
2. The Bake House; built 1762.
3. Modern Wooden Houses.
4. Hot Shot Furnace; built before 1812; rebuilt later.
5. French Magazine; built before 1759.
6. French Barracks; built 1757.
7. Southwest Block House; built 1756.
8. Northeast Block House; built 1756.
9. Life Saving Station.
10. Cemetery.

Part of the 13th Infantry, who came to this place and were in the battle of Queenston, in 1812, are now garrisoning Fort Niagara; and by a singular coincidence, this centennial finds in command of this fort an officer of the same rank, and bearing the same name, though serving under a different flag, as he who commanded it 100 years ago, Col. Smith; at this date Col. Alfred T. Smith, U. S. A.

### A BRIEF SUMMARY.

Such is "a brief history of old Fort Niagara." The spot where it stands has been the scene of many contests, beginning with the days when the redmen resisted the erection of any sort of a fortification here.

It has seen a fort erected and demolished; it has seen rival European nations plotting, striving and contending for its ownership; it has seen, during French rule, the reflection of Parisian life and manners and the horrors of a political prison; it has seen the savages sacking the fort, thieving not butchering, for there was peace between the French and Indians at the time; it has seen the horrors of a siege, and a surrender.

It has seen the ascendency of the English and the unbridled license that their officers of that day gave to their lust and passions. It was during the ownership of both these nations the greatest market for Indian trade — especially in furs and brandy — in the country. To this spot the savages continually flocked, often, yes, very often, bringing with them wretched white prisoners, many of whom, to the credit of both the French and the English, were ransomed by the officers of the fort.

It has seen the most shameless plans prepared here by British leaders and Indian chiefs, the natures of both being as much that of fiends as of men formed in the image of their Maker.

It has seen marauding parties sallying out from here to rob, murder and destroy. It has witnessed bloody strife between the great English-speaking nations of the old and new world respectively.

And to-day the old fort remains, as a relic, but bearing within its ramparts and in the earthworks outside, the standing records of history for at least 150 years back. And with a record back of that, which is somewhat traced in this article for over another hundred years; and back of that still, is an unknown history when this spot of land was owned by the Neuter nation.

84        *OLD FORT NIAGARA IN HISTORY.*

It is sincerely to be hoped that the United States will forever guard and preserve these buildings and the earthworks of the old fort, and not allow them to be razed or restored. They should be allowed to remain intact, as memorials of the history of former generations.

And so, in the belief that I have proved the statement, I close substantially as I began, by asserting that no one spot of land in North America has played a more important part, been more coveted, and exerted a greater influence, both in peace and war, on the control, on the growth, on the settlement, and on the civilization of the country, than the few acres embraced within the limits of old Fort Niagara!

HOT SHOT FURNACE.

www.ingramcontent.com/pod-product-compliance
Lightning Source LLC
Chambersburg PA
CBHW020322090426
42735CB00009B/1370